'What is a philosophical argument?' 'Why accept one philosophical theory rather than another?' The author begins his inquiry by answering these questions. He analyzes different kinds of philosophical argument, always illustrating them with examples from actual philosophical literature, and then provides criteria for rejecting defective philosophical theories outright and criteria for choosing between acceptable, but competing, theories. He then distinguishes six senses of 'a private language' and discusses the question whether or not there can be a private language. This discussion leads to an analysis and disproof of solipsism and to an explication of the concept of mind and an analysis of the mind-body complex. The concept of mind dovetails with the earlier discussion of private languages and provides the basis for forming an intelligible concept of knowledge-of-other-persons. In analyzing this concept, the author shows that the chief ground for philosophers' denying that such knowledge is possible is inconsistent. He concludes the work with a discussion of knowledge and scepticism in which he analyzes certain common concepts of knowledge and, finding them unsatisfactory, proposes an alternative to them.

D1290125

Born in New York City, Mr. Hoffman received the B.A. degree from Brooklyn College and the M.A. and Ph.D. degrees from New York University and has taught at both institutions. He has contributed to numerous periodicals, including *The Australasian Journal of Philosophy*, *Mind*, *The Philosophical Quarterly*, *Philosophical Studies*, and *Sophia*.

LANGUAGE,
MINDS, AND
KNOWLEDGE

Language,
Minds,
and
Knowledge

ROBERT HOFFMAN

Department of Philosophy
New York University

HUMANITIES PRESS

New York   1970

To BONNIE

You, you eternally: you
Ineffable Spring of my life,
River of vehement green
And dream of all enterprise . . .

"I often have long conversations all by myself, and I am so clever that sometimes I don't understand a single word of what I am saying."

"Then you should certainly lecture on Philosophy."

—OSCAR WILDE, *The Remarkable Rocket*

Acknowledgments

Yea, a joyful and pleasant thing it is to be thankful.

—*The Book of Common Prayer*

My interest in the subject of this book was awakened by the writings of Professor A. J. Ayer and stimulated and encouraged by Professor C. J. Ducasse. That I ever reached the point where I was able to undertake the inquiry that issued in this book I owe to the provocative guidance of Professor Sidney Hook. My friends Professor Kai Nielsen and Dr. Sidney Gendin made numerous helpful criticisms of my first draft of this book; and Dr. Gendin was also kind enough to play victim when I occasionally wanted to talk myself through an idea without allowing my listener the consolation of criticism.

During my philosophical and other trials I have fortunately had the friendship of Simon Silverman, Sidney and Natalie Gendin, and Stanley and Susan Malinovich, without which I might have lost heart. I am indebted to my friends Alex Blum and Marvin Kohl for sympathy and encouragement; and to my friends Gary and Sally Cagle for kindness when life frequently seemed to me otherwise unbearable during an academic year I spent in Kansas, and when I myself sometimes was unbearable. I take great pleasure in here acknowledging my gratitude to all these friends.

I am also pleased to take this opportunity to thank my parents not only for making possible my formal education in philosophy but for the many benefits that came of their believing in me even when I could not give them any visible sign of achievement.

Robert Hoffman

Preface

> "Where shall I begin, please your Majesty?" [asked the White Rabbit.]
> "Begin at the beginning," the King said very gravely, "and go one till you come to the end: then stop."
>
> —LEWIS CARROLL, *Alice's Adventures in Wonderland*

This work deals with a cluster of closely related epistemological problems.

I introduce my discussion of these problems with an account of different kinds of philosophical argument. After briefly discussing deductive philosophical argument, I discuss various modes of non-deductive philosophical argument and elucidate a concept of non-deductive proof. I then give criteria for rejecting proposed philosophical theories outright and other criteria for choosing between acceptable philosophical theories.

I then move to the epistemological problems themselves. I examine the contention that since a private language is impossible, the fact that there is language shows that there is a linguistic community and therefore that solipsism is false. After commenting on language in general, I refute the contention by distinguishing six concepts of a private language and showing that those relevant to the contention are self-consistent.

I then explain solipsism in greater detail and examine some arguments for the existence of a reality independent of the putative solipsist's conceptual and perceptual constructions. I offer a criterion for distinguishing myself from the world in which I exist and I conclude that insofar as solipsism is true it is trivial and insofar as it is not trivial it is false.

I next advocate a materialistic conception of mind according

9

to which my having an experience is identical with my being in a certain brain-state or my undergoing a certain brain-process. This theory, which I explain and defend at considerable length, fits nicely with the earlier discussion in which I contend that certain epistemologically important concepts of a private language are self-consistent. It also permits me to provide an intelligible and useful concept of my having knowledge of other persons. In analyzing this concept, I show that the chief ground for denying that such knowledge is possible is itself inconsistent.

I conclude the work with a discussion of knowledge and scepticism in which I analyze certain common concepts of knowledge and, finding them unsatisfactory, propose an alternative to them.

Contents

CHAPTER I

Philosophical Theories

> These are much deeper waters than I had thought.
> —ARTHUR CONAN DOYLE, *Reigate Squires*

> A philosophical work consists essentially of elucidations.
> —LUDWIG WITTGENSTEIN, *Tractatus Logico-Philosophicus*

Discussing what can be inquired into and reasoned about, Hume proposes this test whether or not a work is genuinely informative:

> *Does it contain any abstract reasoning concerning quantity or number?* No. *Does it contain any experimental reasoning concerning matter of fact and existence?* No. Commit it then to the flames: for it can contain nothing but sophistry and illusion.[1]

Elsewhere, Hume writes that it is a mistake to divide all arguments into demonstrative and probable:

> . . . to conform our language more to common use, we ought to divide arguments into *demonstrations*, *proofs*, and *probabilities*. By proofs meaning such arguments from experience as leave no room for doubt or opposition.[2]

I believe that the second of these contentions is correct and, moreover, that philosophical argument ideally aims at establishing conclusions so as to "leave no room for doubt or opposi-

---

[1] David Hume, *An Enquiry Concerning Human Understanding* (1777), 1902, p. 165.

[2] *Ibid.*, p. 56.

tion." I shall explain and illustrate how philosophical argument does this.

There is no doubt that some philosophical statements appear to be incompatible with others. Of course not every pair of statements that appear mutually incompatible are incompatible. The non-philosophical statements 'Chocolate ice-cream is good' and 'Chocolate ice-cream is not good' need not be mutually incompatible if asserted by different people, for these statements usually are to be understood as disguised first-person reports of one speaker's liking or tending to like chocolate ice-cream and the other's not liking or tending not to like chocolate ice-cream. And directly these statements are converted into straightforward first-person reports we see that there is no contradiction in simultaneously asserting them: the first speaker, S_1, states "I like or tend to like chocolate ice-cream", and the secod speaker, S_2, states "I do not like or tend to like chocolate ice-cream". Each statement has a different logical subject, in one instance S_1 and in the other S_2. Substituting the name of the person denoted by 'I' for each occurrence of 'I', we derive 'S_1 likes or tends to like chocolate ice-cream' and 'S_2 does not like or tend to like chocolate ice-cream', which are jointly assertable without contradiction. Similarly, even apparently mutually incompatible statements that do not include value terms may not in fact be mutually incompatible. Thus, although Leucippus, Democritus, and Epicurus assert that atoms are indivisible and a contemporary physicist asserts that atoms are divisible, the two statements are not mutually incompatible, for the strict meaning of the term 'atom' varies with the theory of which it is part. Indeed, in the explanatory discourse of the Greek atomists the statement that the atom is indivisible is analytic, whereas in that of the contemporary physicist it is synthetic. Examples of the sort just given suggest that apparently mutually incompatible statements may not actually be mutually incompatible but may recommend different usages or embody different usages of key terms. Accordingly, philosophical statements should not be taken at face value. It may be that they cannot be understood apart from the arguments that support them. And so, to ascertain whether or not philosophical statements are incompatible with each other we

should look beyond their apparent incompatibility to the arguments that support them.

But the mere fact that the statements are mutually incompatible does not entail that the activity that issues in someone's
making the statements is a rational activity. For a person may
make even plain statements of fact because he is non-rationally
persuaded of their truth. He may believe that Santa Claus exists,
because believing that makes him feel good or because he desires to conform his beliefs to those of the majority of his social
group. Yet if he tells us that either is the reason why be believes
that Santa Claus exists we rightly reject his belief as irrational
or non-rational, though perhaps correct. And if he comes to affirm
all his beliefs the same way, we rightly reject them all as irrational
or non-rational, though they may be correct, and we rightly conclude, moreover, that the activity by which he comes to affirm
them is itself irrational or non-rational.

In philosophy, statements are made that allegedly justify or
prove other statements. When philosophers disagree with an
allegedly justified or proved statement, they do not merely deny
it, but sometimes offer some other statement(s) to justify or to
prove its contradictory. That this is so is *prima facie* evidence that
philosophizing is a rational activity. An acknowledged paradigm
of rational activity is mathematics. One of the common modes of
mathematical proof is the *reductio ad absurdum* argument, according to which the truth of a proposition is established by
showing that its formal contradictory entails a self-contradictory
proposition. Waismann, while admitting that philosophical arguments have force, contends that they are not deductive and
therefore do not prove anything.[3] The tacit major premiss of his
argument is that only a deductive argument can prove anything.
I shall discuss this premiss below. What I want to discuss here
is his minor premiss, namely, that no philosophical argument is
deductive.

---

[3] Friedrich Waismann, "How I See Philosophy", in H. D. Lewis, ed., *Contemporary British Philosophy*, 1956, p. 471. For an illuminating critique of Waismann's notion of philosophic argument, see A. B. Levinson, "Waismann on
Proof and Philosophic Argument", *Mind*, LXXIII, No. 289, pp. 111-116 (1964).

I believe that this premiss is false. Consider the following argument in aesthetics,[4] concerning the ontological status of the work of art, say, of a particular poem. Suppose I want to prove that the poem is not identical with the succession of experiences —sensations, images, feelings, and ideas—that a reader has when he is reading the poem. I want to prove that the poem is not identical with a reader's experiences when he reads it. The structure of my argument is this. (1) Both my opponent and I affirm that the status of exactly one poem is in question. (2) I assume that my opponent's suggestion that the poem is identical with a reader's experiences while reading it is true. (3) As a matter of fact the relevant experiences of different readers of the same poem differ, namely, the experiences of which the poem is the control object. (4) From (2) and (3) it follows that there are as many poems associated with these experiences as there are different sets of experiences. Indeed, each set of experiences is a different poem. But (5), (4) is incompatible with (1). Now, it should be emphasized that when my opponent and I agree that the status of exactly one poem is in question we are using the expression 'exactly one poem' philosophically neutrally. Whatever is denoted by that expression is a pre-analytic datum that limits the philosophical conclusion by requiring that it state that there is exactly one poem, although that poem may be post-analytically understood to be something quite definite, such as the set of ideas the poem's author has when he reads it, or the sign-design of which the copy we read is a sign-event, etc. A pre-analytic datum antedates and determines inquiry, whereas a post-analytic datum postdates and depends upon inquiry. Thus, the argument is a genuine *reductio ad absurdum*. And insofar as my opponent continues to accept (1) and (3), he must reject (2) and accept its formal contradictory, which is what I set out to prove.

Aristotle, in denying the Platonists' belief that there are Ideas, uses a *reductio ad absurdum* argument.[5] He argues as follows. (1) The Platonists believe that the Ideas necessarily are at rest. (2) The Platonists believe that the Ideas are in us. (3) Assume there

---

[4] I discuss this argument in detail in my "Conjectures and Refutations on the Ontological Status of the Work of Art", *Mind*, LXXI, No. 284, pp. 512-520 (1962).

[5] Aristotle, *Topics*, II. 7. 113a.

are such Ideas. (4) It follows from (2) that when we move, the Ideas in us move. But (5), the derivation in (4) is incompatible with (1). Hence, (6), there are no Ideas as characterized by the Platonists.

Unsuccessful attempts to use a *reductio ad absurdum* argument include some of the most famous philosophical arguments. I mention but one. Aquinas' second alleged proof of the existence of God, from efficient causation, proceeds by assuming that there is no single first cause but rather an infinite sequence of causes. These alternatives are allegedly the only possible alternatives; and since the second allegedly turns out not to be possible, the argument concludes by asserting that there must be a single first cause, called God.

In view of the foregoing, what can Waismann mean to deny when he denies that philosophical argument is deductive? He offers essentially one reason to support his contention that philosophy does not contain any deductive argument.

> A first alarming sign can perhaps already be seen in the notorious fact that the ablest minds disagree, that what is indisputable to the one seems to have no force in the eyes of the other. In a clear system of thought such differences are impossible. That they exist in philosophy is weighty evidence that the arguments have none of the logical rigor they have in mathematics and the exact sciences.[6] (471).

I do not believe that Waismann's so-called weighty evidence is weighty. To begin with, notice that he states that arguments in mathematics do have logical rigor. It is clear that he here has a *system* of thought in mind when he writes that philosophy lacks such arguments. He plainly suggests that the differences of opinion that are found in philosophy but allegedly not in mathematics are found in the former but not in the latter because the former is not "a clear system of thought" whereas the latter is. But why this emphasis on a *system* of thought? Much philosophical argument is piecemeal, such as the *reductio ad absurdum*

---

[6] Waismann's rhetoric takes liberties with his logic. The second defining clause of the first sentence should read: "that what is indisputable to the one seems to the other to have no force." If the seeming were *to us* and *about the eyes of the other*, Waismann would not properly have adduced a relevant incompatiblity.

arguments mentioned above. Surely it would be perverse to deny that these arguments are philosophical arguments, that is, that their subjects are philosophical.

Moreover, arguments in some systems of philosophy not only purport to have some of "the logical rigor [arguments] have in mathematics", but in fact have it. Spinoza for instance, whom Waismann mentions only to ignore, claims that his *Ethics* follows Euclid's method. And to some extent it does, differing from it in that whereas Euclid's Propositions always are accompanied by what Euclid calls "figures", which give practical application to the relevant logical deduction, Spinoza's are not. Consider the third and fourth Definitions of the *Ethics*.

> *Substance* is that which is in itself, and is conceived through itself; in other words, that of which a conception can be formed independently of any other conception.
> *Attribute* is that which the intellect perceives as constituting the essence of substance.

From these Definitions, he derives his named Proposition, which is that two substances whose attributes wholly differ have nothing in common. I believe that the derivation is valid. 'Attribute' is here synonymous with 'predicate' and, for the purpose at hand, 'substance' may be taken as that in which properties inhere or that of which they are constituted. Attributes are what we know of substance. Now, suppose there are two substances. According to Spinoza's definition of 'substance', we can form a conception of each of them without forming one of the other, which is to say that they are not linked conceptually. We form a conception of each substance by knowing its attributes. And so if, *ex hypothesi,* the two substances have no attribute in common, they have nothing in common. For the only sense it makes to speak of them having something in common is to assert that they have this or that attribute in common. As I wrote above, I believe that Spinoza's Proposition II is validly derived from the aforementioned Definitions of his system. To be sure, Spinoza's system may include very many logical blunders; but that is no reason to deny that his system is deductive or to assert that none of his derivations is valid.

Finally, if difference of opinion about the validity of allegedly proved conclusions is the mark of a non-deductive or non-rigorous system of thought, then mathematics is such a system. I quote but one author.

> In the whole [mathematical] literature, from Euclid to Bourbaki in-clusive, there are scarcely any proofs in the logical sense. The number of original books or papers on mathematics in the course of the last 300 years is of the order 10^6; in these, the number of even close ap-proximations to really valid proofs is of the order 10^1. Thus the chances of finding a mathematical publication that contains even one genuine proof are less than 1 in 10,000; and since most publications contain many so-called "proofs," the proportion of legitimate proofs to the whole number offered as such is negligibly small. It is remarkable in view of this, that so many mathematicians pride themselves on what they call their "logical rigor."[7]

Quite beside this author's belief, the intuitionist critique of math-ematical proof is such as to show that whether a putative math-ematical proof is acceptable or not is a matter about which there is disagreement among the ablest minds. In non-intuitionist math-ematics, which accepts the law of the Excluded Middle, a con-sequence of that Law is that the falsity of the falsity of a proposition p entails the truth of p. Thus, a proof that the square root of two is not a rational number proceeds by showing that the assumption that the square root of two *is* a rational number leads to a self-contradiction. But in intuitionist mathematics this "proof" is not acceptable. For although the intuitionist rejects any proposition that entails a self-contradiction, since he does not here accept the Law of the Excluded Middle, he cannot legit-imately infer that the square root of two is not a rational number from the proposition that it is false that the square root of two is a rational number.

Admittedly, there is less disagreement in mathematics than in philosophy. But then, so far as disagreement is concerned, the difference between them is quantitative, not qualitative. And Waismann himself admits that philosophical arguments have force, despite their allegedly not proving anything. This admis-sion makes it seem as though his intent is to recommend a linguistic reform, namely, that since sound philosophical argu-

---

[7] P. H. Nidditch, *Introductory Formal Logic of Mathematics*, 1957, pp. 1-2.

ments, unlike sound mathematical arguments, need not be deductive, we should not call both types of arguments "proof", lest someone be misled into rejecting forceful philosophical arguments merely because they are not deductive. Rather, we should say that sound mathematical arguments prove their conclusions, whereas sound philosophical arguments merely persuade us of theirs. But is this recommendation wise? Is not more lost than gained if we state that philosophical argument does not prove its conclusion? Waismann justifies the recommendation by the statement that only deductive argument proves its conclusion and by the following statements.

> . . . arguments . . . must contain inferences, and inferences must start somewhere. Now where is the philosopher to look for his premises? To science? Then he will "do" science, not philosophy. To statements of everyday life? To particular ones? Then he will never be able to advance a single step beyond them. To general statements? If so, a number of questions raise their ugly heads. By what right does he pass from 'some' to 'all'? Can he be sure that his premises are stated with such clarity and precision that not a ghost of a doubt can creep in? Can he be sure that they contain meat, are not analytic, vacuous, definitions in disguise and the like? Can he be sure that they are true? (471)

I want to inquire into whether or not only a deductive argument proves its conclusion. Of course, if 'proof' is defined as a true statement that a certain proposition is entailed by a certain other proposition(s), then by definition only a deductive argument proves its conclusion. But the definition makes it seem that conclusions supported some other way necessarily are not conclusive. I propose to show that this appearance is delusive and that the suggested definition of 'proof' which gives it ought therefore to be rejected.

Consider the following hypothetical conversation between a woman and her husband in which she rationally persuades him of something.

W. (Signifying one of two paintings) Buy that one.
H. But it costs more.
W. I know. But it's not every day we buy a painting; and we both prefer that one and the price is not very much greater.
H. Okay, we'll buy it.

I think we may properly call the wife's argument an ordinary-language proof, that is, an instance of the kind of proof that frequently is offered and accepted in everyday affairs. There is a rational relationship between the wife's "But . . . greater" and the conclusion that she and her husband should buy the painting. Her argument is not the sort of thing we should have if she had said, "The artist's surname has eight letters, so let's buy his painting." or "Cloudy weather is forecast for tomorrow, so let's buy this painting." The facts that the expenditure is not an everyday expenditure, that the difference in price is not very great, and that they both prefer the same painting are relevant to their buying the painting, whereas neither the number of letters in the painter's surname nor the weather forecast for tomorrow is relevant to their buying it. Lest someone conclude that the wife's argument therefore is really an enthymeme, which is a deductive derivation with a suppressed premiss, I want to emphasize that this conclusion distorts the meaning of 'enthymeme'. The tacit premiss of an enthymeme is obvious, whereas whatever tacit premiss the wife's argument has, if any, is not obvious. "He's reading Plotinus, so he must be a muddle-headed scholar" is an enthymeme with the obvious tacit premiss, "Only a muddle-headed scholar reads Plotinus", but the wife's argument has no similarly obvious tacit premiss. Surely it would be a mistake to contend that her argument includes the tacit premiss "Buy whichever painting we both prefer, provided it's not very much more expensive than the highest priced alternative painting and we don't buy a painting every day". It would be a mistake because the suggested tacit premiss falsifies the original argument and is itself too imprecise to ground a deductive proof. How often is 'every day' and how much more expensive is 'very much more expensive'? And even if this question can be answered precisely, the added premiss would not be exceptionless. It could be controverted, for instance, by the true statement, "But we're heavily in debt" or "But we need whatever money we have to pay our rent". Stating the suppressed premiss of a genuine enthymeme strengthens its conclusion, for the resulting deductive argument explicitly states all that is needed to establish the conclusion. But stating the alleged suppressed premiss of the wife's argument does not strengthen its conclusion. Indeed, it weakens it. The resulting deductive argument is weaker because to see that it is valid we should need to know under precisely what conditions the prescriptive premiss holds or is controverted. Merely to state that premiss with the additional tacit provision 'Other things being equal' is to render the wife's argument vacuous. For there are infinitely many logically possible conditions each of which may controvert the premiss, so the premiss cannot function as the basis of a deductive proof. The wife's argument is more cogent as an ordinary-language proof, for her rationally supported conclusion stands until legitimately criticized. And to criticize it legitimately, its critic must have some rational ground for doubting it, some statable objection to her judgment that she and her husband ought to buy the painting. Of course, nothing in my argument is intended to deny that the wife's argument can be converted into a deductive argument if we arbitrarily stipulate some allegedly suppressed premiss. My point is that any allegedly suppressed premiss can be shown to suffer from the defect from which the aforementioned candidate suffers or merely to be so implausible as to distort the wife's original argument.

I have stated that the wife's reasons rationally persuade her husband that they should buy the painting. But someone may admit this and yet deny that her argument is a proof. I have not yet explained what I mean by calling it a proof. I shall now explain. For an argument to be an ordinary-language proof, its justificatory statements must be reasonably believed to be true and there may not be any criticism of the conclusion that cannot be answered in the light of knowledge available in the circumstances in which the proof is offered. The first requirement is the evidence-requirement and the second requirement is the criticism-requirement. Thus, if someone carefully and deliberately avoids being near any black cat because he believes he will die directly one touches him, though he has no evidence of any person ever having died because that person was touched by a black cat, then we rightly say that he has no proof because he has no evidence whatever. His argument fails to satisfy the evidence-requirement. Next, consider the situation in which an anti-religious fanatic, like the atheist, Joseph Lewis, contends that he knows that Jesus of Nazareth is a fiction because although historians have investigated the question of Jesus' historicity, no honest historian asserts that there is any evidence of his historical existence. Suppose that when we adduce the controverting evidence or apparently genuine historical documents by non-historians of the first century A.D. in which Jesus frequently is mentioned in reports of events occurring in Galilee and Jerusalem, the anti-religious fanatic is unable to show that the documents are spurious. Then we rightly reject his alleged proof that Jesus is a fiction because his argument fails to satisfy the criticism-requirement.

Consider one more ordinary-language proof. This one is even simpler than the other. Suppose I see someone go into a room that I know to have no exit but the doorway by which he enters. Suppose I station myself directly outside this doorway, fix my eyes on it, and do not notice him leave. Then I have sufficient grounds for saying that he is still in the room. The statement 'He is still in the room' is proved. In this example, unlike the former, there is no testimony by any person; the evidence is direct, being entirely first-hand. But, as formerly, the attempt to make this proof an enthymeme by alleging it to contain a suppressed premiss is misguided. Adding the allegedly suppressed premiss, 'Whoever goes into a room having only one exit and is not seen to leave by that exit although the exit is continuously visible from the time he enters, is still in the room', distorts the argument because this premiss can easily be controverted and therefore needs an 'other things being equal' clause. Controverting statements, if true, are 'The person observing the exit sees, but does not notice, the person leave the room' and 'The person in the room disguises himself and then leaves the room unrecognized', etc.

This concept of ordinary-language proof entails the legitimacy of saying that someone can prove what is not so, which is a linguistically deviant statement. I believe it is linguistically deviant just because the notion of proof *qua* valid deductive argument to a true conclusion is far and away the most common concept of proof. But this concept can be criticized on two grounds. First, mathematical arguments, the paradigm of deductive proof, are not really proofs but derivations. Notice that in the second passage quoted from Waismann's paper, he suggests that philosophical arguments are not proofs because the philos-

opher cannot be sure that the premisses of his arguments are true
or even that they are not vacuous. But if this is his ground for
denying that philosophical arguments are proofs, he should
equally deny that mathematical arguments are proofs. For the
premisses of mathematical arguments are not true statements but
analytic statements or definitions in disguise. Waismann's reasons
for denying that philosophical argument can be deductive really
are reasons for denying that any argument whatever is a proof.
Second, there is no reason why the justificatory statements of a
proof need be *known* to be true in the sense of being beyond
every possible doubt. It is enough that they be *reasonably
believed* to be true, that is, be beyond any reasonably believed
objection in the doubting situation. Indeed, although no argument can prove its conclusion by establishing it beyond all
possible doubt, an argument may prove its conclusion in that,
at the time the argument is asserted, its justificatory statements
are unexceptionable so far as the scope of our actual knowledge
is concerned and so its conclusion is warranted by them. This
concept of proof is tantamount to an argument's passing the test
of actual criticism. The conclusion is not guaranteed against all
possible criticism but only against the errors that satisfactorily
answered criticism alleged to be present. Future criticism may
be unanswerable, and so the proof may turn out to be defective
relative to it. But if an argument is unassailable so far as we can
tell, then it proves its conclusion so far as we can tell. To the
contention that perhaps future criticism may show that it is
defective, it is sufficient to reply that perhaps future criticism
will not show that it is defective. Even if it were to show that
that the argument is defective, it is possible that additional future
experience will show that the criticism itself is unsound. In short,
the question whether or not an argument is a proof is time-
dependent, for the putative evidence of an indeterminate future
is itself indeterminate.

I think there can be no doubt that philosophers sometimes
attempt ordinary-language proofs of their theses. Here are three
examples of putative ordinary-language proof in philosophy. I
shall not here discuss the soundness of the first two. The first one
is by Austin and attempts to prove that there is no special kind
of sentence that is *as such* incorrigible and that so-called material

object statements can be known as certainly as so-called sense-data statements. He writes:

> If I carefully scrutinize some patch of colour in my visual field, take careful note of it, know English well, and pay scrupulous attention to just what I'm saying, I may say, 'It seems to me now as if I were seeing something pink; and nothing whatever could be produced as showing that I had made a mistake. But equally, if I watch for some time an animal a few feet in front of me, in a good light, if I prod it perhaps, sniff, and take note of the noises it makes, I may say, 'That's a pig'; and this too will be 'incorrigible,' nothing could be produced that would show that I had made a mistake.[8]

The second putative ordinary-language proof is by Flew and purports to prove that it cannot be right to say that no one *ever* acts of his own freewill, because the meaning of 'of his own free-will' can be taught by reference to such paradigm cases as that in which a man, under no social pressure, marries the girl he wants to marry. And such paradigm cases, according to Flew, are not specimens that might have been wrongly identified, for they are what 'acting of one's own freewill' is.[9]

This last example is an instance of a sub-type of ordinary-language proof frequently used in contemporary philosophy, namely, the paradigm case argument. Briefly, it consists in arguing that since the meaning of some expressions is taught by reference to cases or instances of the expressions' denotations, there must in principle be at least some instances of the denotations. An excellent example of this argument is Stebbing's argument purporting to prove that Eddington's and Zimmer's contention that neither a plank of wood nor a piece of paper is a solid object is mistaken.[10] Against their contention Stebbing

---

[8] J. L. Austin, *Sense and Sensibilia*, 1962, p. 114. Austin may here be sanctioning philosophers' using this type of proof rather than using one himself.

[9] Antony Flew, "Philosophy and Language," in Antony Flew, ed., *Essays in Conceptual Analysis*, 1956, p. 19. Flew is sanctioning a type of philosophical proof and gives the freewill argument as a paradigm of the type.

[10] A. S. Eddington, *The Nature of the Physical World*, 1929, pp. x-xi, 342; Ernest Zimmer, *The Revolution in Physics,* trans. by H. Stafford Hatfield, no date, p. 51; L. Susan Stebbing, *Philosophy and the Physicists* (1937), 1958, pp. 51 et seq.

argues that unless we understand 'solidity' we cannot understand what the denial of solidity amounts to and that we *can* understand 'solidity' only if we can truly say that the plank of wood and the piece of paper are solid. For 'solid' is the very word we use to describe a certain respect in which these objects resemble each other and a block of marble and a cricket ball, and in which each of these differs from a sponge, from the interior of a soap-bubble, and from holes in a net. So if the plank is non-solid and the piece of paper is non-solid, then we do not even know what 'solid' *means* and therefore are in no position to deny that anything is solid.

I believe that the paradigm case argument is not a strong argument, though it is useful. The contention that the meaning of an expression is taught by reference to paradigms is ambiguous, being either a psychological proposition about how we come to know what the expression means or a philosophical proposition about what the meaning of the expression is. If the former, then the proposition is irrelevant to whether or not the expression is correctly applied. For no matter how we learn the meaning of an expression (perhaps by having electric current passed through our brains or by taking drugs!), we may or may not correctly apply it. The fact that we learn its meaning one way rather than another is conceptually independent of the fact that its meaning is such-and-such. If the contention is that the paradigm case argument is a contention about what the meaning of an expression is, then it embodies a mistake. Neither a plank of wood nor a piece of paper, for instance, need have been pointed to as a paradigm of solidity for us to have learned the meaning of 'solid'. If Stebbing's contention is that what is *meant* by 'solid' is 'of the consistency of such things as planks of wood or pieces of paper', then her contention is false, for what is meant by 'solid' has no particular reference to planks of wood or pieces of paper. If her analysis were correct, then 'This plank of wood is solid' and 'This piece of paper is solid' would be analytic statements, which they clearly are not.

The second interpretation seems to be what the paradigm case argument comes to, namely, that since there are or were standard examples to which an expression is or was applied, that expression is meaningful and its meaning is exemplified by those examples. Hence, to say that a plank of wood or a piece of paper is not solid is absurd. But this contention overlooks the fact that even if we do learn the meaning of 'solid' by having planks of wood and pieces of paper pointed out to us, it does not follow that these things are solid. I may learn the meaning of 'orange' by having not only orange things pointed out to me, but by having things of clearly approximate colors pointed out to me in contradistinction to things of obviously non-approximate colors, for instance, things of deep chrome yellow, apricot, cherry, and geranium in contradistinction to green things and blue things. But the things of the four approximate colors eventually cease to function as paradigms of 'orange'. Similarly, planks of wood and pieces of paper, in contradistinction to sponges, may serve as paradigms when we learn the meaning of 'solid' and yet later be revealed by an Eddington or a Zimmer to be porous. Here 'solid' has the meaning 'non-porous' and Eddington and Zimmer contend that even if we conceive of sub-atomic particles as being substantial they are scattered specks in regions mostly empty. Eddington remarks, however, that "if we eliminated all the unfilled space in a man's body and collected his protons and electrons into one mass, the man would be reduced to a speck just visible with a magnifying glass" (1-2). This speck would of course be solid. The obvious difference between these two examples is that in the former we actually perceive some red thing, whereas in the latter we do not actually perceive any solid thing. But this difference is beside the point. Eddington and Zimmer have a meaning for 'solid', namely, 'non-porous'; and so it makes perfectly good sense to deny that the plank of wood and the piece of paper are non-porous and to affirm that only a pure mass of protons and electrons, could we get it, would be non-porous. The paradigm-case argument makes a valuational leap from *applying* an expression to a given thing to *correctly applying* that expression to the thing. But 'E is applied to T' does not entail 'E is correctly applied to T'. Thus, to apply 'solid' to something, it is enough to believe that it is non-porous; but what is believed to be non-porous may nevertheless be porous. What modern physics allegedly shows, according to Eddington and Zimmer, is just this, that things generally believed to be non-porous, such as planks of wood and pieces of paper, in fact are porous. Their contention may be false, but it is not absurd. In fact it is neither. Stebbing's argument against their contention is irrelevant to it. Ordinary-language, as I shall argue in detail below, is not philosophical discourse. Notice that their contention does not include a denial that a plank of wood or a piece of paper *appears* to differ in the relevant respect from a sponge. Their contention is that appearances are here deceptive. Hence, Stebbing's statement about how we ordinarily use the relevant expressions, whose ordinary-language use is learned from acquaintance with *appearances,* scarcely can justifiably be expected to prove Eddington and Zimmer wrong. Stebbing and others who use the paradigm case argument this way confuse the O.E.D. with 'Q.E.D'.

Someone may object that Eddington is mistaken, for if 'solid' has any meaning at all, then surely a plank of wood is just the sort of thing that is solid. Indeed, one is tempted to ask, "If *it* is not solid, then what would be?" But to ask this is to fail to observe that Eddington states quite clearly what would be solid, namely, the logically possible collection of particles that constitute the plank. And what he states is perfectly intelligible. Moreover, when the paradigm-case advocate points to a plank and asserts, "What we mean by 'solid' is this plank . . . ", his statement is a meta-linguistic statement about 'solid'. Call it S. S is equivalent to T, the object-linguistic statement, "This plank (again he points to it) . . . is solid". But T is just what Eddington denies. Clearly, then, Stebbing cannot validly *refute* Eddington's statement merely by assuming the truth of its formal contradictory, which is what she does. In short, her argument and arguments like hers beg the question.

I have explained why I believe the paradigm-case argument is not a strong argument, but have not yet explained why I nevertheless regard it as useful. Notice that even when I criticized Stebbing's use of it to try to disprove the Eddington-Zimmer contention, I appealed to it insofar as the meaning of 'porous' was concerned. One type of philosophical argument is the contention that an expression is discriminatively intelligible if, and only if, it has an intelligible contradictory. Ths contention is sometimes called the principle of non-vacuous contrast. It states that over any range of things, no predicate can function discriminatively and yet not contrast with some other predicate at least in principle. 'Wise', for instance, cannot function discriminately unless some other predicate does, so that the concept not-wise is intelligible. 'Stupid' is such a predicate. For the application of a predicate to be discriminatively legitimate according to this principle there need not actually exist a member of the denotation of the contrasting predicate, but there must be one at least in principle. To show that the Eddington-Zimmer sense of 'solid' is discriminatively intelligible, I contrasted it with the meaning of 'porous', which we all accept. Since 'porous' is intelligible and since 'solid' means 'non-porous', their contention is not absurd, as Stebbing says it is, but intelligible. I contrasted the expression whose intelligibility is questioned with an expression whose intelligibility is granted, and argued that in the relevant context they function as contradictory predicates and so are both intelligible. Ordinary-language here furnishes one of the three plausible justificatory statements of my argument. The argument can be formulated as follows.

1) (The Principle of Non-Vacuous Contrast): If one term is intelligible and another term is the negative of the first term, then the second term is intelligible.	Definition.
2) The Principle of Non-Vacuous Contrast is true.	Assumption.
3) 'Porous' is intelligible.	Ordinary-language.
4) 'Solid' means 'non-porous'.	Eddington-Zimmer.
5) 'Solid' is intelligible.	From 3) and 4), by 1) and 2).

Ordinary-language discourse is fundamental to philosophy only in that it is the discourse by means of which philosophical discourse deviates from the ordinary-language usage. In the Eddington-Zimmer contention, for instance, it is by referring to the ordinary-language expression 'porous', the intelligibility of which is not denied, and by using ordinary-language discourse that the physicists state their deviant 'solid'. Moreover, there is a sensible presumption of correctness of the linguistic usage that has traditionally been made do for whatever we have wanted to distinguish in human experience. But insofar as a *specific* expression is concerned, this presumption may be set aside by newly discovered facts or by new insights into the significance of already known facts.

Passmore, after distinguishing different kinds of self-refutation that appear in philosophical argument, contends that only one is conclusive. He writes that "formally, the proposition *p* is absolutely self-refuting, if to assert *p* is equivalent to asserting *both p and not-p.*"[11] It is important to notice that *asserting* both p and not-p is required for there to be an absolute self-refutation. 'Both p and not-p' in itself is not absolutely self-refuting, for it may appear in a logic text as an example of the form of a certain kind of statement, or in a grammar text as an example of the form of a certain kind of sentence. Such an occurrence of 'Both p and not-p' is not self-refuting because it asserts nothing whatever and so, *a fortiori*, nothing incompatible with any other assertion it also makes. Passmore maintains that the absoluteness of an absolute self-refutation consists in the fact that such a refutation permits no evasion of any kind. But this criterion is inconsistent with the requirement that for p to be self-refuting it must be asserted. Since 'assertion' means 'strong or assured affirmation' and since, accordingly, assertion is properly used only by persons having certain thoughts or intentions, someone not having the relevant thoughts or intentions about p but nevertheless saying "I assert p" makes an utterance that is an abuse of the practice of asserting and that therefore is something less than an assertion. An example of this is an average child's repeating his physicist-father's words: "I assert that a molecule is formed by two atoms only if each atom can contribute an electron with a free spin." To be sure, that 'I assert' is a pure explicit performative suggests that to pronounce it *is* to assert. But as Austin shows, even the utterance of a pure explicit performative may be infelicitous, as

---

[11] John Passmore, *Philosophical Reasoning*, 1961, p. 60. Cf. however, J. L. Mackie, "Self-Refutation—A Formal Analysis", *The Philosophical Quarterly*, 14: 193-203 (1964).

in my example.[12] Hence, that the user of p prefaces it by 'I assert' does not eliminate the possibility that he is guilty of an infelicity. And since p itself does not indicate how p is being used and since the user's declaration that he really is asserting p may be false, it is possible to evade the alleged self-refutation that Passmore regards as absolute.

My purpose so far has been two-fold, to show that there are kinds of non-deductive proof used in philosophical argument and to show that if one analyzes disproof by alleged absolute self-refutation carefully and minutely enough he sees that the alleged absoluteness is delusive. I have wanted to show these things so that when I state what I believe may reasonably be asked of philosophical argument there will be a background of different kinds of philosophical argument against which my statement may be appraised. And to this end I shall discuss still other kinds of philosophical argument.

I mentioned that Passmore distinguishes different kinds of self-refutation, only one of which he alleges to be absolute. He lists two others, pragmatic and *ad hominem*, which I shall now briefly discuss. A pragmatic self-refutation consists in a statement's falsity being established entirely from the fact that the statement is made as it is, as when someone *says* 'I cannot speak'. If he were to *write* 'I cannot speak', his statement might be true; but it is necessarily false when he utters it. Strictly speaking, it is not the *proposition* 'I cannot speak' that is self-refuting, nor the *operation* of someone's saying 'I cannot speak', but the operation's occurring prefixed to that particular content. Passmore, however, does not believe that there is any absolute self-refutation here, for he admits a possible evasion. The person

> could reply that he had a small gramophone concealed on his person; knowing he would some day lose his voice, he had spoken these words on to a record, which he now played in order to announce his dumbness. Since it is, very obviously, always an empirical question whether a person . . . has uttered a certain statement, it will follow that he can always—in principle, even if sometimes with almost inconceivable hardihood—deny that he has in fact . . . uttered the statement. (63)

---

[12] J. L. Austin, *How To Do Thing With Words*, 1962. See page 18 for a table of infelicities and *passim* for their explanation.

Passmore is here guilty of an equivocation on 'say' and of making an irrelevant point even if sound. The person using the small concealed gramophone does not utter the words 'I cannot speak,' but plays his gramophone which causes sounds to be emitted that are like those he would make if he could speak as he did when he recorded them. He now "says" he cannot speak, not in the relevant sense of *speaking*, but in the irrelevant sense of *making known*. But this is unimportant, for Passmore makes his point independently of the gramophone example, namely, that it is an empirical statement, so denial that he did is not logically self-contradictory.

Passmore cites Descartes' *cogito* argument as a putative proof by pragmatic self-refutation, with Descartes arguing that he can establish beyond doubt that he is a thinking being, since for him to doubt that he is a thinking being is for him to think he is not thinking and so to be a thinking being. Passmore correctly points out that for Descartes to establish his conclusion he must not only say that he thinks he is not a thinking being but must show his saying that to involve his thinking. For if when he says that, someone denies his assertion on the ground that he cannot think but can only say he thinks, he has no adequate reply. Clearly there is no logical necessity that anyone who speaks must first have thought. And since Descartes does not show that a person who says "I think that I am not a thinking being" or, more narrowly, "I am thinking that I am not thinking" *always* is in fact thinking when or immediately before he says this, his *cogito* argument is not even a pragmatic self-refutation.

The *ad hominem* self-refutation does not consist in the *fact* that the relevant statement is made as it is, but in an *admission* the asserter makes during the course of making his assertions. He admits that something is so which, if it were so, would be inconsistent with at least one of his other assertions. Passmore's example of a putative *ad hominem* self-refutation in philosophy is an argument of Socrates' in the *Theaetetus:* Protagoras is alleged to teach the doctrine that "no one can inform anybody of anything" and therefore to be guilty of an inconsistency. For if the doctrine is true, he cannot teach it; and if, as he himself contends, he can teach it, the doctrine is false. Passmore rightly emphasizes, however, that Socrates must show that to teach is to inform, or there is no self-refutation. If he does, Protagoras must either withdraw his doctrine, or deny that he teaches it to anyone, or be inconsistent.

The charge of self-refutation can be evaded, no matter which kind of self-refutation is charged, because for there to be any kind of self-refutation, a proposition must be asserted. And as I have shown, whether or not a proposition is asserted is an empirical question to which a negative answer always is possible. Of course, that such an answer is possible does not mean that it should be given in every instance. And so we may properly use self-refutation as a mode of argument provided we keep in mind that the beliefs we reject because they entail allegedly self-refuting propositions may be sound and that the probability that they are sound is identical with that we affix to the statement that the putative self-refutation is itself refutable.

A philosophical contention sometimes is rejected because it embodies or entails an infinite regress. But not all infinite regresses are vicious and so not all infinite regresses should be avoided. Russell distinguishes two kinds of infinite regress.[13] In the objectionable one, two or more propositions jointly constitute the *meaning* of some proposition; and of the constituents, the meaning of at least one is similarly compounded; and so on *ad infinitum*. The non-objectionable infinite regress is one of perpetually new implied propositions, each having a definite meaning and the first implying the second, the second implying the third, and so on *ad infinitum*. Only in the first kind of regress does the expression to be defined reappear in the definition itself and thereby vitiate the process by precluding its arriving at a proposition that has a definite meaning. In the second kind there is no logical necessity to complete the regress before the expression generating it acquires a meaning, which putative completion is of course impossible.

An example of the difference between the two kinds of infinite regress is two interpretations of an argument of Ryle's. He discusses "the intellectualist legend" about intelligent behavior, according to which "whenever an agent does anything intel-

---

[13] Bertrand Russell, *The Principles of Mathematics*, 2nd edit., 1937, pp. 50-51, 99-100, 348-349. Cf. George Edward Moore, *Commonplace Book 1919-1953*, ed. Casimir Lewy, 1962, p. 109.

ligently, his act is preceded and steered by another internal act of considering a regulative proposition appropriate to his practical problem",[14] and he inquires whether or not we must, on this account, say that before the agent can reflect how to act to be intelligent he must first reflect how to act intelligently to reflect.

> The crucial objection to the intellectualist legend is this. The consideration of propositions is itself an operation the execution of which can be more or less intelligent, less or more stupid. But if, for any operation to be intelligently executed, a prior theoretical operation had first to be performed and performed intelligently, it would be a logical impossibility for anyone ever to break into the circle. (30)

There are two interpretations of "the intellectualist legend", according to one of which Ryle's argument is cogent and according to the other of which it is not. If the legend purports to define 'intelligent action', but in doing so employs the very notion of intelligent action, then the proposed account of intelligent action is worthless. But if the legend purports merely to assert the psychological hypothesis that intelligent action is preceded by intelligent reflection, then Ryle's argument is worthless. The first interpretation yields the objectionable kind of infinite regress, whereas the second interpretation yields the unobjectionable kind of infinite regress.

One of the most forceful kinds of philosophizing does not as such include argument at all. Its aim is not to argue for a thesis but to eliminate bias or perplexity, or sometimes to generate perplexity so as to lay the groundwork for argument. Often we are thrall to linguistic forms; and this kind of philosophizing aims to set us free: where linguistic forms dominate our thinking, we are to dominate the forms. The best example I know of this sort of philosophizing is Wittgenstein's attack on essentialism, specifically on the question, 'What do diffrent language-games have in common that entitles them to be called language-games?' He believes that there is no property common to all, but that they are related to each other by a complicated network of similarities, which he calls their family resemblances. He does not argue this point by discussing the network of resemblances, but rather tries to break the hold of the "common noun-common property" legend

---

[14] Gilbert Ryle, *The Concept of Mind*, 1949, p. 31.

that dominates our thinking. He does this by giving examples of family resemblances elsewhere, viz., where we talk about games, members of a family, weaving, numbers, and plants.[15]

Another good example of this kind of philosophizing is Austin's attack on the doctrine that all present tense indicative sentences express statements of fact or descriptions. He offers numerous examples that create perplexity, which his detailed argument later removes: to say "I name this ship the Queen Elizabeth" (while smashing the bottle against the stem) is to name the ship, not to report that I am naming it; to say "I bet you sixpence it will rain tomorrow" is to bet, not to report betting; etc.[16]

This kind of philosophizing is best regarded as a species of elucidation, rather than as a species of proof. Its watchword is "Do not say 'such-and-such must be the case', but look and see what the facts are." And to assist us to see what the facts are, examples are presented to illustrate little noticed or usually ignored facts or to emphasize that in general the relevant facts are more numerous or more complex than our dominant linguistic forms lead us to believe. Often we assume something before we consider it sufficiently. The question about "what is in common", for instance, wrongly assumes that members of a class must have a common property in virtue of which they are members of that class, and the thesis that Austin attacks assumes wrongly that present tense indicative sentences can be used to express only one sort of statement. Wittgenstein's and Austin's elucidations give us a profounder understanding of language and orient us to features of experience that differ from those it is usually used to discriminate.

A complete philosophical theory is a rational discourse about the world or some part of it. It consists of a body of coherent and general analyses of certain kinds of phenomena, for instance, sensing, perceiving, understanding, believing, knowing, etc. The phenomena just mentioned are epistemological phenomena and the analyses of them constitute epistemological discourse. Since a philosophical theory consists of analyses, it must include descriptions of the phenomena it analyses. And such descriptions

---

[15] Ludwig Wittgenstein, *Philosophical Investigations,* esp. Secs. 65-71.
[16] J. L. Austin, *How To Do Things With Words,* pp. 4f.

should be philosophically neutral in the sense of not committing anyone who accepts them to accept or to reject any particular analysis or philosophical terminology.

That such a neutral description can be stated is questioned by several philosophers. Hanson,[17] for instance, contends that there is an important sense in which seeing is a theory-laden undertaking. Observation, he contends, is dependent upon prior knowledge and so describing what we see also is theory-laden. For if our prior knowledge of something conditions our selection and organization of the constitutive features of the thing, then our description of these features, and so of the thing, allegedly varies with our prior knowledge. Hanson illustrates his contention that seeing is theory-laden with miniature accounts of how Brahe and Kepler would *see* the increasing distance between the horizon and the sun.

> Tycho sees the sun beginning its journey from horizon to horizon. He sees that from some celestial vantage point the sun (carrying with it the moon and planets) could be watched circling our fixed earth. Watching the sun at dawn through Tychonic spectacles would be to see it in something like this way.
>
> Kepler's visual field, however, has a different conceptual organization. Yet a drawing of what he sees at dawn could be a drawing of exactly what Tycho saw, and could be recognized as such by Tycho. But Kepler will see the horizon dipping, or turning away, from our fixed local star. The shift from sunrise to horizon-turn . . . is occasioned by differences between what Tycho and Kepler think they know. (23-24)

Put quite succinctly, Hanson's contention is that although Brahe's and Kepler's eyes are similarly affected, they describe their experiences differently. Although their retinas, if normal, bear the same impression, so that if each could perfectly represent his impression their drawings would be congruent, Brahe would say that he sees the sun rise, whereas Kepler would say that he sees the horizon drop. Thus, *seeing* is theory-laden; or put slightly differently, interpretations are built into descriptions.

Against the contention that the sun "appears to both of them to be rising, to be moving upwards, across the horizon", Hanson

---

[17] Norwood Russell Hanson, *Patterns of Discovery*, 1958.

quotes Frank's remark that "our sense observation shows only that in the morning the distance between horizon and sun is increasing, but it does not tell us whether the sun is ascending or the horizon is descending" (182). But Hanson misses part of the import of this remark. To be sure, the remark does show that the descriptions of Brahe and Kepler are theory-laden. But what are we to say of Frank's description of the observed situation? Is it too theory-laden? Surely not. Frank's description, to wit, "in the morning the distance between horizon and sun is increasing", is neutral between the theories of Brahe and Kepler. Indeed, Hanson himself seems to admit this when he admits that the same thing dominates their visual attention (7). For he is arguing that what dominates their visual attention is described differently by each because the description each offers embodies an interpretative or explanatory element. But he cannot intelligibly state that the *same* thing dominates their visual attention unless he can describe the alleged "same thing" in language that is not theory-laden. For only if Brahe and Kepler would agree that a certain description describes a specific thing could they or anyone else know that their theory-laden descriptions are of that thing. Accepting the same description is necessary to accepting the thing described as the same thing.

The descriptions that are part of philosophical theory need not be of actual fact, but may be of hypothetical situations. To see how a description may fail by not being philosophically neutral, consider the following argument by Malcolm.[18] He examines the alleged ordinary usage of 'know' in a hypothetical situation in which several of us intend to go for a walk in Cascadilla Gorge, but he protests that he wants to walk beside a flowing stream and that at this season the gorge is dry. He writes:

> You say "I know that it won't be dry" and give [the] reason, e.g., "I saw a lot of water flowing in the gorge when I passed it this morning." If we went and found water, there would be no hesitation at all in saying that you knew. If, for example, we later met someone who said "Weren't you surprised to see water in the gorge this afternoon?" you would reply "No, I *knew* that there would be water; I had been there earlier in the day." We should have no objection to this statement. (59)

[18] Norman Malcolm, *Knowledge and Certainty*, 1963, pp. 58ff.

On the contrary, I object very strongly to the relevant statement, for I believe that no one would make it unless he were being provocative or pompous, or were talking *philosophically*. Otherwise he would reply without using the 'I *knew*' clause, by saying simply "No, I was there earlier today." Malcolm should realize this, for he writes that there would be no hesitation in saying that the person knew, and so makes a philosophical point about whether or not it is philosophically proper to say that someone can now know the truth of a proposition about the future. Given the statement about there being no hesitation in saying that the person *knew,* then if Malcolm's usage were not theory-laden there would not be any point in emphasizing that the person knew. What Malcolm does is to impose a philosophical usage of 'know' on the hypothetical situation and so to misdescribe what would happen in ordinary circumstances. This done, he then justifies his philosophical usage by referring to the putatively accurate and acceptable description. What he does is, of course, unsound just because the theory he advocates is already assumed by being built into the description. He could have avoided this error by deleting the 'I knew' clause from the hypothetical conversation and by stating instead that the person knew there would be water in the gorge. Of course, whether or not Malcolm's contention about someone's now knowing that a proposition about the future is true needs to be argued for in either event.

Given that the descriptions in two philosophical theories are philosophically neutral, what makes one theory better than the other? There are three kinds of reason why such a theory should be rejected outright and two kinds of reason why one such theory should be preferred to another. A proposed theory should be rejected outright if (1) it is incoherent, (2) it is refuted by an experiential datum, or (3) it is incompatible with well-grounded scientific theory; and a proposed theory should be preferred to another acceptable theory if (4) it is simpler than the other theory, or (5) it is more comprehensive than the other theory. Brief examples of each kind of reason are in order.

First, consider a theory of personal identity according to which the criterion of personal identity is the disposition to recall having had certain experiences. If, for instance, someone awakes with the memories associated with being the historical Socrates and is able to describe hitherto unknown but subsequently confirmed events in Socrates' life, then we should properly regard that person (or the single person who then occupies just that body that reports the memory experiences) as identical with the Socrates who is mentioned by Plato and Xenophon and whose trial is reported in Plato's *Apology*. This theory of personal identity is incoherent, since if one person can awake with such a disposition, so can two or more persons awake with it, and if they do, the theory commits its proponent to identify each of them with Socrates and thereby to assert that Socrates is more than one person (or that his person then occupies more than one body), which *ex hypothesi* is false. The theory commits us to assert both that Socrates is exactly one person and that he is not exactly one person.

Second, suppose that someone adequately describes the type of experience produced by works commonly called works of art and proceeds to propose a theory of the nature of a work of art on the basis of analyses of works that cause him and others to have an experience of the appropriate kind, the occurrence of the experience being the criterion by which he decides whether or not something is a work of art. Suppose the sample on which his theory is based leads him rightly to propose a theory that excludes from the category of art works any verbal work that does not make some moral point. If he encounters a new verbal work, for instance a haiku poem, that does *not* make any moral point but that *does* produce the relevant experience, then he should reject his theory as proposed. For by his own criterion, the new work is a verbal work of art.

Third, suppose there is a theory of physical causation that is based on the mechanistic concepts of classical physics according to which atoms and sub-atomic particles are regarded as being like extremely tiny billiard balls. This theory in incompatible with well-grounded contemporary physical theory, for according to Heisenberg's Uncertainty Principle we cannot identify particles at the sub-atomic level because a discontinuity is introduced into sub-atomic phenomena by the interaction between the particles and the process of sub-atomic observation. Since we cannot identify these particles, it makes no sense to speak of physical causation among them as we speak of physical causation among identifiable macroscopic objects. And so a theory of the nature of physical causation that ignores quantum physics should be rejected as *ipso facto* deficient.

Fourth, of two philosophical theories neither of which is to be rejected for a reason of any of the foregoing kinds, the theory to be preferred is whichever is simpler. Consider first a brief non-philosophical example.[19] Suppose that two people who have just moved into a neighborhood are known to be related to each other, that the nature of their relationship is not known, and that two hypotheses concerning it, both based entirely on hearsay, are entertained, viz., H^1, that they are father and son, and H^2, that they are brothers. Now suppose that we see the two people and notice that they look the same age, which piece of evidence fits well with H^2 but not with H^1. H^1 need not be surrendered, however, for it may be supplemented by the auxiliary hypothesis A^1, that the putative father is a very vain man who by various means has succeeded in reducing his apparent age well below his real age. But this suggestion makes H^1 slightly more complicated than H^2. Suppose, further, that we talk with the putative father and find that he does not seem vain in conversation. This piece of evidence counts against A^1, which, however, may be saved by the additional auxiliary hypothesis A^2, that he is a shrewd person who takes pains in conversation to conceal his vanity. By the addition of this hypothesis (and others that it entails), H^1 becomes considerably more complicated than H^2. In contrast to H^2, which does not require any auxiliary hypothesis for it to unify the phenomena that need to be explained, H^1 requires several auxiliary hypotheses. Accordingly, H^2 is so much simpler than H^1 that H^2 should be accepted rather than H^1, for the theory that is easier to defend in the long run is preferable.

A philosophical example of the relevant sort of simplicity is the following. Assuming that both materialism and occasionalism are acceptable philosophical theories of causal interaction between so-called physical events and so-called mental events, then materialism is simpler and therefore preferable, because it does

---

[19] This example was suggested by one in G. Schlesinger, *Method in Physical Science*, 1963, p. 37.

not need to introduce the concept of God's effecting changes when so-called causal interaction occurs between the events.[20]

Fifth, of two philosophical theories neither of which is to be rejected for a reason of any of the foregoing kinds, the theory to be preferred is whichever is more comprehensive. In general, one theory is more comprehensive than another if it covers more facts than the other. Thus, field theory, which covers the facts covered by two completely different branches of physics, electromagnetism and optics, is more comprehensive than either of those branches of physics. Less obviously, one theory is more comprehensive than another if its assertions are more precise than those of the other, for the more precise its assertions are the more numerous its assertions are. To see what is meant by this dependence of numerousness of assertions on precision of assertions, consider another non-philosophical example. Suppose a measured quantity is reported first as 7.4 and then more precisely, in the light of further measurement, as 7.43. Now, the more precise measurement permits us at least one additional assertion, namely, the assertion that the measured quantity is not only 7.4 but 7.43. This assertion not only permits additional comparison with other equally precisely measured quantities, if any, but in itself is more informative than its predecessor. For measurement to hundredths has ten times the falsifying power of measurement to tenths since it allows only one tenth as much deviation as the less precise measurement. Any hundredth place digit will confirm the 7.4 measurement, but only a 3 in the hundredth place will confirm the 7.43 measurement.

Two philosophical examples of a theory's being preferable because more comprehensive than its alternative are the following. First, assuming that both materialism and vitalism are philosophical theories neither of which is to be rejected for a reason of the foregoing kinds, then materialism is more comprehensive and therefore preferable, because it enables us to formulate a conceptual scheme of the behavior of both living organisms and nonliving matter, whereas vitalism enables us to formulate a

---

[20] See Harold Cherniss, "The Philosophical Economy of the Theory of Ideas", *American Journal of Philology*, LVII (1936), for an illustration of the importance of simplicity in assessing a philosophical theory.

conceptual scheme of only living organisms. Second, assuming that phenomenalism conceived as the reduction of all terms to the names of sense-experiences is intelligible, then phenomenalism is less comprehensive than realism in that no epistemological discourse consisting entirely of proper names and expressions designating combinations of proper names can be used to go beyond immediate experience, whereas realism can be so used because it includes general terms.

The last example shows that the ideal of simplicity and that of comprehensiveness sometimes conflict. When they do, and relative simplicity and relative comprehensiveness are the only points of difference upon which the choice between two philosophical hinges, how should we choose between them? I do not know how to answer this question, for I cannot provide a criterion for choosing between them. I believe that the choice simply varies with individual philosophical taste and that one philosopher may prefer a simpler but less comprehensive theory to a less straightforward but more comprehensive theory, whereas another philosopher may prefer the latter theory to the former. This non-rational choice is restricted to a special case, however, and should not be permitted to obscure the fact that philosophical argument is rational and that, in general, there are rational grounds on which to prefer one philosophical theory to another.

CHAPTER II

Public Language and Private Language

> It does not matter, of course, what a sentence is called as long as we know what the facts are and how they are to be explained.
>
> —Jaakko Hintikka, *Knowledge and Belief*

A quite general question relevant to epistemological discourse is: "Can there be a private language?" In his contribution to a symposium on that question Rhees writes:

> When we talk about something, our language does not point to it, nor mirror it. Pointing or mirroring could refer to things only within a convention, anyway: only when there is a way in which pointing is understood and a way in which mirroring is understood. I point for the sake of someone who understands it. Apart from that it were an idle ceremony; as idle as making sounds in front of things.[1]

Although any attempt to state the implication of these contentions for the epistemology of perception would be irrelevant to Rhees' paper, the implication is there to be drawn. Allegedly, speaking a language is possible only if there are rules of usage. These rules, moreover, are possible only within a community of users of the language. Accordingly, if someone speaks a language, there must be some other person who understands the language. No one can consistently contend both that he speaks a

---

[1] R. Rhees, "Can There Be a Private Language?", *Belief and Will*, Aristotelian Society Supp. Vol. XXVIII, 1954, p. 77.

language and that solipsism is true. For if he speaks a language, he must be a member of an at least two member linguistic community; and the other member must be an entity whose linguistic behavior is independent of the putative solipsist's will, to which extent the other member himself necessarily is independent of the putative solipsist's will. In short, then, there cannot be a language unless there is some perceptual entity whose behavior is independent of the speaker's control.[2]

There are, however, many senses of the key expression 'a private language'. What I propose to do, therefore, is to state different senses of this expression and to analyze the resulting concepts of a private language, thereby ascertaining whether or not they are self-consistent.

PRIVATE LANGUAGES:

1) An experiential language the expressions of which are meaningful to its user without any of them actually having been translated into another language.
2) An experiential language at least one of whose designative expressions does not signify any intersubjectively perceivable entity.
3) An experiential language none of whose designative expressions signifies any intersubjectively perceived entity.
4) An experiential language some of whose expressions convey information to a non-user but that do not convey the same information to him as to the user.
5) An experiential language some of whose expressions convey information to a non-user but that cannot convey the same information to him as to the user.
6) An experiential language none of whose expressions can be understood by a non-user.

The importance of keeping these distinct can be seen in the fact that philosophers writing on the subject of a private language may begin by defining 'a private language' in one sense and then argue that a private language is possible in quite another. Thus, in a recent article[3] the author begins by defining a private

---

[2] Cf. N. P. Tanburn, "Private Languages Again", *Mind*, LXXII, No. 285, pp. 88-89 (1963).

[3] William Todd, "Private Languages", *Philosophical Quarterly*, 12: 206-217 (1962).

language as one that it would be logically impossible for anyone other than the user to understand (p. 206) and concludes that there can be a private language because if the user "did not already know a public language he could learn one in the usual way and then compile a notebook in which, opposite each sentence in the private language, there would be its correlate in the public language" (p. 217). But the author has here begun with sense 6) and ended with sense 1). Any person whatever who speaks the public language will be able to understand the private language as soon as he thoroughly familiarizes himself with the completed notebook. But this means that the only sense in which the private language was private before the correlation is that it had not yet been translated into another language, not that it was untranslatable into another language.

It is advisable to discuss the concept of a natural language before analyzing the concepts of a private language. A natural language is a system of dispositions to perform certain speech acts,[4] mainly to communicate and to co-ordinate activities among the members of a group. The elements of the language are certain sounds that are produced by members of the group to act as stimuli upon other members of the group and so to influence their behavior. Only *certain* sounds will do, however, for the natural language is systematic or rule-governed. The rules are of two general kinds, syntactical and semantical. Syntactical rules are formation rules in accordance with which sounds are combined; and semantical rules are rules in accordance with which sounds signify things and in accordance with which combinations of sounds satisfy the non-syntactical conditions that must be satisfied for the performance of a speech act to occur.

But just what is a rule? One common kind of rule is the regulation. Such a rule has an author and a history—that is, it is enacted by someone at a certain time, continues unchanged for a certain duration, and may be modified or revoked at some other time. A rule of this kind has a force in that it indicates whether a certain class of actions is obligatory, forbidden, or permissible. Traffic regulations and regulations governing membership in

---

[4] There are other sorts of communications, e.g., writing, mimicry, etc., but these are substitutes for the conventional use of vocal sound.

associations are instances of this kind of rule. And although it is
not known who invented chess or precisely when it was invented,
chess rules are paradigmatic of the kind of rule we are discussing.
Thus, the rule regulating the bishop is: 'Each bishop may move
from its square only in its diagonal provided it encounters no
obstruction.'

Wittgenstein likens a word to a chess piece:

> The question "What is a word really?" is analogous to "What is a
> piece in chess?"[5]

The likeness is reinforced by Wittgenstein's likening language to
a game:

> Systems of communication . . . we shall call "language games."
> They are more or less akin to what in ordinary language we call games.
> Children are taught their native language by means of such games,
> and here they even have the entertaining character of games. We are
> not, however, regarding the language games which we describe as in-
> complete parts of a language, but as languages complete in themselves,
> as complete systems of human communication.[6]

But Wittgenstein recognizes that the analogy is limited, for he
writes:

> Let us recall the kinds of case where we say that a game is played
> according to a definite rule.

---

[5] Ludwig Wittgenstein, *Philosophical Investigations,* 2nd edit., 1958, Sec.
108. There are several philosophers to whom the be-all and the end-all of
philosophy seem to be what Wittgenstein would say, said, or would have said.
Since I am not writing a biography, I have no interest whatever in what he
would say if he were alive. And since I am not writing an account of his philosophy, I have almost no interest in what he would have said had certain statements been put to him. Since I am writing philosophy, I am interested in what
he said only insofar as what he said illuminates my subject. The illumination is
limited by his having stated various theses but no complete theory. The conceptual excellence of his *Philosophical Investigations* consists in its striking,
puzzling insights into the problems with which it deals. But these insights are
insights of problem-stating, not of problem-solving. Wittgenstein wanted his
writing "to stimulate someone to thought of his own", not "to spare other people
the trouble of thinking." The *Philosophical Investigations* is a work admirably
designed to succeed in this; and it is not Wittgenstein's fault certain neo-Wittgen-
steinians will not let it.

[6] Ludwig Wittgenstein, *The Brown Book,* 1958, Sec. 5.

The rule may be an aid in teaching the game. The learner is told it and given practice in applying it.—Or it is an instrument of the game itself.—Or a rule is employed neither in the teaching nor in the game itself; nor is it set down in a list of rules. One learns the game by watching how others play. But we say that it is played according to such-and-such rules because an observer can read these rules off from the practice of the game—like a natural law governing the play.[7]

First, Wittgenstein is wrong, or at least inaccurate, when he likens a word to a chess piece. If language and chess are games, then what should be likened to a chess piece is a sentence, not a word. The unit of linguistic meaning relevant to a language is its sentences. Isolated words and phrases are meaningful only in the derivative sense of occurring in sentences that are meaningful.

Second, the rules of chess can be stated antecedently to the game's being played. Someone can have the bishops pointed out to him, be told where to position them so that the game can begin, and then be given the rule 'Each bishop may move from its square only in its diagonal provided it encounters no obstruction.' The practice of moving a bishop is instituted by the statement of that rule. The rule is stated prior to any instance exemplifying its application. Can the rules of a language be stated prior to all the instances of their application? Clearly some rules of a language can. Thus, in English the expression 'Let 'vixen' denote female foxes', which is a rule obliging users of English to use 'vixen' only if they thereby refer to female foxes, might have been stated prior to all instance of so using 'vixen'. But this rule could not be stated or understood unless the rules of usage governing 'Let . . . denote . . .' were understood. Any statement of a rule necessitates that the person who promulgates the rule understand the rules of usage governing the expressions used to state the promulgated rule. Let us call the rules of a language that can be stated prior to all instances exemplifying them 'derivative rules' and those that cannot 'basic rules'. Clearly the rule about 'vixen' is a derivative rule and the rule 'Let . . . denote . . .' is a basic rule. Now, a basic rule does not have an author

---

[7] Ludwig Wittgenstein, *Philosophical Investigations*, Sec. 54.

or a history in the language in which it is stated. Rather, it co-exists with the language. Hence, it is not a regulation.

Perhaps a basic rule is a uniformity of some sort. The word 'rule' sometimes denotes a mere uniformity, as when we say: 'As a rule, wills must be witnessed.' Consider Wittgenstein's statement:

> One learns the game by watching how others play. But we can say that it is played according to such-and-such rules because an observer can read these rules off from the practice of the game—like a natural law governing the play.

Watching someone play chess we may see that the bishops move diagonally and never beyond an occupied square, and so we analyze this chess-behavior by formulating the rule 'Each bishop may move from its square only in its diagonal provided it encounters no obstruction.' But by formulating the rule we not only note a uniformity in the chess-behavior, we deny that the chess-behavior is an accidental uniformity and imply that it is a specimen of conformative act. But why should we exclude accidental uniformity? Because there are peculiar signs in the players' behavior, such as an opponent's refusal to move until the person who moved the bishop in non-conformity to the rule has moved it in accordance with it, or perhaps such a refusal coupled with an emphatic pointing to an occupied square that has been passed over, etc.

We read the rule from the practice of the game, like *a natural law* governing the play. The likeness to which Wittgenstein points is appropriate. In regarding something as a rule of chess we regard it as general, not as limited to any particular game or situation. Thus, if we state the bishop-rule in the form of a general proposition 'Every B is R' (short for 'Every chess-bishop is a piece that may move from its square only in its diagonal provided it encounters no obstruction.'), we understand that proposition to entail of a game still in progress during which all four bishops have been captured that if any of them had not been captured it would be R. Notice the likeness to Braithwaite's definition of 'natural law':

> A true contingent general proposition "Every A is B" whose generality is not limited to any particular relations of space or of time will be

called by a person C a *law of nature* or *natural law* if either the corresponding subjunctive conditional "Although there are no A's, yet if there were any A's they would all be B's" is reasonably believed by C, or this subjunctive conditional would be reasonably believed by C if he were reasonably to believe that there are no A's. . . . In addition all true hypotheses containing theoretical concepts will be given the title of natural laws.[8]

A further statement in Braithwaite's account of 'natural law' is instructive:

The condition for an established hypothesis *h* being *lawlike* (i.e. being, if true, a natural law) will then be that the hypothesis either occurs in an established scientific deductive system as a higher-level hypothesis containing theoretical concepts or that it occurs in an established scientific deductive system as a deduction from higher-level hypotheses which are supported by empirical evidence which is not direct evidence for *h* itself.[9]

Reading the bishop-rule off from the practice of the game is not merely noting a uniformity. For the peculiar behavioral signs associated with errors having been made are taken as marks of the players' intention or desire to behave a certain way. Their behavior is regarded as intentional or motivated behavior in the sense of involving their heeding what they are doing. Whether their behavior is believed to be preceded by some occult cause or is believed merely to involve thinking (in contradistinction to being habitual), understanding their behavior is believed to require something more than simply enumerating instances of bishop-moves. And the "something more" is a hypothesis containing theoretical concepts either of occult causes or of dispositions.

However, that the players want to behave a certain way may erroneously lead us to believe that they must be aware of the rule to which their behavior conforms. It is quite possible that they themselves be unaware of the rule. Thus, although it is not a rule of chess to do so, certain players may always say 'gardez' when they expose their opponents' queens to immediate capture and may reproach each other for failing to say it in these circum-

---

[8] Richard Bevan Braithwaite, *Scientific Explanation*, 1953, p. 301.
[9] *Ibid.*, pp. 301-302.

stances. Their behavior when exposing an opponent's queen to immediate capture is structurally identical with their behavior when exposing an opponent's king to immediate capture. Nevertheless, they may never state the rule that a player is to warn his opponents when he exposes his opponent's queen to immediate capture. Suppose, however, that if some observer were to suggest to them that they have been following such a rule they would admit they had been and would not alter their chessbehavior after the suggestion had been made. Then they would have been observing an implicit rule that became explicit when it was brought to their attention.

Notice that very few utterances made in a natural language get their meanings stipulatively. 'Roger', for instance, is an interjection that originally was arbitrarily selected to signify that a message had been received and understood, being short for '(message) received (and understood)'. It is still used as an interjection having that meaning. Similarly, 'positron' was coined from '*posi*tive' and 'elec*tron*' to denote the sub-atomic particle having an equal but opposite electrical charge to an electron's and the same mass, spin, and lifetime as an electron's. And 'blurb' was coined arbitrarily and has retained its meaning of 'a brief extravagant commendatory notice of a book, such as its publisher would be likely to write to increase sales'. Usually, however, the rules of usage for the utterances of a natural language are read off from the practice of speaking the language.

First, there is the ostensive use of a sentence. Someone may learn the meaning of the utterance 'red' ostensively. Thus, a native speaker of English construes 'red' as a one word sentence short for 'This is red.' and exposes the learner to a line of different-colored balls of the same size, only one of which is red. The native speaker removes only the red ball from the line and when he returns it he changes the relative linear positions of the balls. When he removes the red ball he utters 'red', but not otherwise. The identical size of the balls ensures that the learner will not take 'red' to indicate the size of the removed ball; and changing the relative linear position of the red ball ensures that he will not take 'red' to indicate the position from which the ball is removed. Thereafter a system of rewards is introduced according to which the native speaker rewards the learner only for uttering 'red' when he removes the red ball. A supplementary system of punishments may be introduced according to which the native speaker punishes him only for uttering 'red' when he removes any other ball.[10] This differential behavioral response to the learner's linguistic response ensures that the learner will not take 'red' to indicate merely that the removed object is a ball or is removed. After he has mastered the technique of using 'red' only when the red ball is removed from the line, other-colored balls than those in the line are added, giving him a greater range of colors from which to distinguish red. Whereas he may begin with three balls, one red, one green, and one blue, the second group may include in addition an orange ball and a pink ball, and the third group may add to these an English vermilion ball and a henna ball. The method of learning the meaning of 'red', however, remains constant.

The meaning of an utterance may be learned less primitively by hearing the utterance used as part of a non-ostensive sentence. This sort of learning presupposes that the learner already know some of the language in which the unfamiliar utterance occurs. Take the sentence 'Granite is harder that feldspar.', which some-one ignorant of geology hears geologists utter. As a speaker of (layman's) English he finds the utterance puzzling because granite and feldspar are equally unyielding to pressure from his fingers. He may ask people whether or not *they* can feel that granite is harder than feldspar, and their answers will confirm his own belief that granite is not harder than feldspar. He may then notice that when geologists use the expression 'harder than' they have not previously felt the objects of comparison to ascertain this, but have tried to scratch one with the other. Thus, a geol-ogist trying to ascertain the mineral content of a rock may say: "I suspect that there is granite in the rock, so I'll see whether or not I can scratch this piece of feldspar with the portion of the rock I suspect to be granite." Being unable to scratch it, he says: "It's not granite, because granite is harder than feldspar." Hear-ing this, our linguistic learner assigns a different meaning to 'harder than' from the meaning he hitherto believed it to have.

---

[10] On p. 54 I shall discuss the question "How would he know that he is expected to utter anything at all?"

Just what the new meaning is he does not yet know. But further inquiry reveals that the importance of the scratching that immediately precedes utterances of 'harder than' is this: A mineral is said to be harder than a second mineral if it scratches the second mineral but the second mineral does not scratch it. Here, the meaning of the utterance 'harder than' has been learned by abstraction, as a fragment of whole-sentence utterances.

Yet another way the meaning of an utterance may be learned is by the learner's getting a description of the denoted object in language familiar to him. Thus, the meaning of 'atom' is modeled on descriptions of billiard balls, and dust particles, and the like. We are told that an atom is an extremely tiny unit of matter, and for instance that the size of the tungsten atom is one hundred millionth of an inch. So that we understand just how small a unit of matter the tungsten atom is we may be given the following information and analogy: "The breadth of a hair is 10,000 times smaller than the length of an outstretched arm (one meter). 100 million is 10,000 times 10,000. Hence the size of the tungsten atom is to the size of one inch as the breadth of a hair is to ten kilometers (six miles)."[11] If similar statements are made about the atoms of other substances, we come to understand that the utterance 'atom' refers to a bit of matter so tiny as to be invisible to the naked eye.

Can the meaning of a basic rule of a language be learned any of these ways, namely, stipulatively, ostensively, contextually, or descriptively? It has already been remarked that a basic rule does not have an author or a history and so is not a regulation, which fact seems to exclude the possibility of learning it either of the first two ways. We have seen, moreover, that some contextually learned rules of a game, for instance the 'gardez' rule of chess, are implicit rules. Hence, that there is no actual statement of a basic rule of a given language does not indicate that the language has no such rule. On the other hand, in our 'gardez' example, once the observer reads the implicit rule off from the practice of the game, he can state it. But a basic rule of a language, such as 'Let . . . denote . . .' seems to be unstatable in that language because to state it one must understand the rules of usage gov-

---

[11] Victor F. Weisskopf, *Knowledge and Wonder*, 1963, p. 85.

erning the expressions used to state it, and these rules of usage seemingly cannot be understood without using the basic rule to explain them. To understand 'Let . . . denote . . .' we should need already to understand the rules of usage governing 'Let . . . denote . . .' Thus, if listening to people speak English leads us to hypothesize the implicit rule 'They have certain utterances denote certain things', how are we to explain what we mean by the expression 'denote'? We cannot meaningfully say "Let 'denote' denote . . .", for unless we understand 'denote' when it occurs in that sentence, we shall be unable to understand it when it is mentioned in that sentence. It seems, then, that we cannot learn the meaning of a basic rule of a language contextually.

Perhaps, however, we can learn its meaning by using two or more learning methods together. Listening to native speakers of a language we may realize that certain sounds are invariably associated with certain things under certain conditions. Thus, we may notice that certain sound-events are of the same sound-design, that certain photochemical effects are of a distinctive type, and that these effects occur only under conditions of a certain kind. Recognizing that the sound-events are of the same sound-design, that the photochemical effects are of a distinctive type, and that these effects occur only under conditions of a certain kind is a basic and unalyzable feature of our perceptual experience. Once this basic recognition is complete, we posit a one-to-one correspondence between a sound-event and the ordered pair consisting of a distinctive photochemical effect and its conditions of occurrence. Of course, this posit does not express a denotative relationship, but only a structural relationship. Clearly, then, there is no way to state additionally that the posited correspondence is a denotative relationship, for to state that, we should need already to understand what a denotative relationship is. It seems, therefore, that we cannot understand the meaning of a basic rule of a language, such as 'Let . . . denote . . .'

But we do use that rule in English, so we must understand it. Perhaps we have shown only that there are uniformities of linguistic behavior that cannot be rationally initiated by the agents, but must arise non-rationally, if at all. Earlier I promised to discuss the (now relevant) question 'How does the person who ostensively learns the meaning of 'red' know he is expected to

utter anything at all?' This question embodies an error. It commits the fallacy of complex question by assuming that the learner
does know he is expected to utter a sound when a certain act of
the teacher's results in the learner's having a certain experience.
But he does not know he is expected to utter a sound nor does he
even believe he is, unless he is familiar with some language before
he begins to learn the meaning of 'red'. If he is, he may believe
the new language parallels the language he already speaks. But
if he is not, if for instance he is an infant, then he can neither
know nor believe he is expected to perform any linguistic act.
For he does not yet know what it would be for him to perform
a linguistic act, since he knows no language with which to perform it. This is not, however, to say he cannot make sounds whose
occurrences in certain linguistic contexts and under certain empirical conditions would constitute his performing a linguistic
act. Just as humans and other primates engage in non-linguistic
imitative behavior, so humans engage in linguistic imitative behavior. And by 'imitative behavior' I mean the copying of a novel
or otherwise improbable act or utterance, or some act for which
there is clearly no instinctive tendency.[12] Linguistic imitative
behavior clearly is not denotative, since at the outset of learning
no stimulus is *definitely* correlated with the learner's response.
Indeed, since 'response' connotes a fairly strong correlation, we
should speak instead of emittance patterns some of which are
imitative. If the linguistic imitative behavior is reinforced by
rewards and then channeled by a system of rewards and punishments, such as employed in the colored-ball language game, the
infant is taught to make utterances conforming to the rules of the
language he is learning to speak. Using sounds to denote things
is a practice non-rationally originated in imitative emittance
patterns and developed by trial and error in conjunction with a
system of rewards and punishments. The proper explanation of
denotative behavior is causal, not linguistic.

    We may now inquire which of the concepts of a private lan-
guage mentioned at the beginning of this chapter are self-consistent.

    The first concept of a private language is that of a language

---

[12] W. H. Thorpe, *Learning and Instinct in Animals*, 1956, p. 122.

the expressions of which are meaningful to its user without any
of them actually having been translated into another language.
There can be a private language of this sort. A code that is not
a mere transcription of a natural language but includes wholly
invented expressions is a private language of this sort. Such a
private language can in principle be translated into another language, though in fact it has not been translated.

The second concept of a private language is that of a language
at least one of whose designative expressions does not denote any
intersubjectively perceivable entity. This designative expression
would denote an experience only of the user's. Wittgenstein
writes:

> Let us imagine the following case. I want to keep a diary about
> the recurrence of a certain sensation. To this end I associate it with
> the sign "S" and write this sign in a calendar for every day on which
> I have the sensation.[13]

"S" is here supposed to function as a name, which Wittgenstein
imagines himself defining ostensively by concentrating his attention on the sensation and naming it S. If he succeeds in naming it,
then the next time he becomes aware of the same sensation he
will call it S and again write 'S' in his diary. But suppose that
some time after he has named the sensation he again experiences
it and accordingly writes 'S' in his diary. Can he know he has
used 'S' correctly? He can if he has a criterion of correctness. But
according to Wittgenstein, he has no criterion of correctness. It
just *seems* to him that the two sensations are the same; and so he
believes he cannot talk about 'correct' in this context. Believing
that a sensation is the same as one he had previously is not like
believing that a man is the same man he saw previously. If he
believes that someone now in his study is the same man he saw
in his study yesterday, there is a criterion independent of his impression or belief that the man is the same by the application of
which he can ascertain whether or not he is. Fingerprints, for
instance, are such a criterion. If there is no criterion of correctness, then Wittgenstein cannot know whether to say of a given
sensation, "This is S", or to say of it, "This is not S". And if he

---

[13] Ludwig Wittgenstein, *Philosophical Investigations,* Sec. 258.

cannot know this, then 'S' is not a name, for what allegedly is named is not identifiable.

But suppose having a sensation is identical with having a certain brain-state or undergoing a certain brain-process.[14] If this is true there is no reason why there could not be a criterion of the sort Wittgenstein requires, and so a private language of the sort we are discussing. Although having the brain-state or undergoing the brain-process is not an intersubjectively perceivable *entity*, it is necessarily connected with something that is intersubjectively perceivable, to wit, the brain-state or brain-process. On this identity theory, the identity obtains between a person's having a certain sensation and his brain's being in a certain state or its undergoing a certain process. This state or process is intersubjectively perceivable. Psychological predicates applying to a person are, on this theory, materially equivalent to physical predicates applying to his living body. The psychological predicates and the physical predicates refer to the same thing. Wittgenstein's 'S' would refer to the same thing to which some description of the condition of his brain refers. The sensation would not be identical with anything physical, but *having the sensation* would be identical with his brain's *being in a certain state or undergoing a certain process*.

This identity theory dissolves the so-called problem of privacy connected with the second kind of private language. Whatever 'S' refers to is private to one person; specifically, it is *his* being in some brain-state or undergoing some brain-process. At this point someone may object that although when I have a certain sensation it is logically impossible that I should be unaware that I have it, it is not logically impossible for me to be unaware of the condition of my brain, and hence that there is no sensation the having of which is identical with any brain's being in any state or undergoing any process. This objection, however, is fallacious, for it rests on a confusion between extensional and intensional contexts. The identity theory asserts that the condition of having a certain sensation (which condition we shall call C) is identical with the condition of some brain's being in a state or undergoing a certain process (which condition we shall call B).

---

[14] I shall defend this theory at length in Chapter Four.

The theory asserts, in short, that C is identical with B. That C and B are identical is contingent, not logically necessary, so someone may *know* something is a C without *knowing* it is a B. The identity statement 'C is identical with B' does entail the statement 'If I am in C then I am in B', but notice that this is an extensional context for 'C' and 'B'. In the statement 'If I know I am in C then I know I am in B', 'C' and 'B' occur in an intensional context. But since neither 'C' nor 'B' is said to be all or part of the meaning of the other, the intensional statement does not follow from the contingent identity of C and B.

Still, someone may object that it makes no sense to speak of the identity of C and B, because for this identity to obtain there cannot be any extensional property x such that 'Cx' is true and 'Bx' is false or vice versa. But in fact a so-called introspective report of a sensation does differ from a physicalistic report of a brain-state or brain-process. I may speak, for instance, of having a pain sensation in my right arm but of having the allegedly identical brain-state or brain-process in my head. Hence, place-predicates applicable to a sensation may differ from those applicable to the allegedly identical brain-state or brain-process. And this being so, the alleged identity does not obtain.

The reply to this argument is that it is based on a misstatement of the identity theory. I am perfectly willing to admit that the argument establishes that at least some sensations are not identical with any brain-state or brain-process, but in admitting this I should emphasize that *this* lack of identity is beside the point. For I never contended that such an identity obtained for *sensations*. What I contended is that a person's having a certain sensation is identical with his brain's being in a certain state or its undergoing a certain process. The objection to which I am replying confuses a sensation with having a sensation and confuses a brain-state or brain-process with being in a brain-state and undergoing a brain-process, respectively. To be sure, a sensation of pain may be locatable in my right arm, whereas a brain-state or brain-process is locatable in my head. But neither having the one nor being in or undergoing the other can be located any more precisely than in the place at which the relevant body is located. Once the body is located, then the *having* and the *being in* or *undergoing* are conditions of that body and occur wherever it is.

One of the statements made in discussing this identity theory is that some philosophers contend that when someone has a sensation it is logically impossible for him not to know he has it. According to these philosophers, if I am in pain I must know I am in pain and so my first-person statement reporting my being in pain, 'I am in pain', is incorrigible, provided I make it without having a slip of the tongue and without intending to deceive anyone. Moreover, these philosophers believe that this incorrigibility attaches also to any other first-person report of a present experience. Since it is but a short step from this contention to the contention that these reports are about private psychic entities and to consequent puzzles about whether or not someone other than the person having the experience can know what the experience is, it is advisable briefly to discuss the belief that first-person reports of present experience are incorrigible.

Suppose I look into a tachistoscope and see a picture of a leopard that has a determine number of spots, and that I then try to state what I have seen. If my look is very brief I may be unable to state how many spots the leopard has and my doubt would be about the content of my own experience. There are two replies to this criticism. First, it may be argued that my statement about the leopard is *not* a report about my present experience but about my past experience and that it is my memory that introduces the element of unreliability into my report. This reply, however, is self-defeating, for no report anyone makes of a so-called present experience is contemporaneous with his having the experience. There always is some time lapse between having an experience and reporting the content of the experience—even so bare an experience as can be correctly reported by 'square red patch now.' Hence, if the time lapse is said to change the leopard-report to a statement about my immediate past and thereby to introduce an element of unreliability, then no statement can be the report of a present experience and every so-called report of a present experience is unreliable the way my leopard-report is or simply is a mis-statment of fact because it is made in the present tense. The second reply is that the content of my leopard-experience is itself indefinite. By this is meant that not all the spots are clearly distinct from those adjacent to them and so my uncertainty about how many spots the leopard has is due neither to the unreliability of my memory nor to my uncertainty about the content of a quite determinate experience, but to the indefiniteness of the experience itself. If I were a sufficiently skillful painter, I should be able to paint exactly what I report and there would be an indefiniteness in the painting. Ayer's analysis of the question whether mistakes about one's own immediate experience are only verbal overlooks this point. In his example, he supposes[15] that he is uncertain whether to say either of two lines of approximately the same length looks to him to be longer and he emphasizes that since he is not uncertain about the meaning of the English expression 'looks longer than' but in fact knows quite well how to use that expression, he is not sure whether either of the lines does *look to him* to be longer than the other. He continues:

> But if I can be in doubt about this matter of fact, I can presumably also come to the wrong decision. I can judge that this line looks to me to be longer than that one, when in fact it does not. This would indeed be a curious position to be in. Many would say that it was an impossible position, on the ground that there is no way of distinguishing between the way things look to someone and the way he judges that they look. After all he is the final authority on the way things look to him, and what criterion is there for deciding how things look to him except the way that he assesses them? But in allowing that he may be uncertain how a thing looks to him, we have already admitted this distinction. We have drawn a line between the facts and his assessment, or description, of them. (69-70)

Here the relevant experience may be indefinite, a point Ayer overlooks. I assert, therefore, that doubt about the precise content of an experience is not itself a good reason to believe we can be mistaken about the content.

But doubt about the precise content of a definite experience, such as a tachistoscopic exposure of the picture of a leopard that has a determinate number of clearly delimited spots, would be another matter. Suppose such an exposure occurs. The advocate of the incorrigibility thesis about first-person reports of present experience cannot now reply that the content of the experience is itself indefinite or vague. The last sentence in the passage

---

[15] A. J. Ayer, *The Problem of Knowledge*, 1956 (Macmillan), p. 69.

quoted from Ayer's book makes an important distinction that is relevant here, to wit, the distinction between facts and the description of those facts. There is a difference between being acquainted with something and being able to describe it. The former is a determinate experience whereas the latter is a classificatory judging of that experience. Thus, I may apprehend the numerousness of the clearly delimited spots without being able to judge that there are exactly forty-five of them. The sensations a person has are connate accusatives of the having but alien accusatives of the describing.[16] The distinction is this. Verbs sometimes take nouns in the accusative case as their objects. Derivatively, then, we may speak of the parallel relationship between the process denoted by the verbs and the things denoted by the nouns. Thus, we may speak of 'jumping a jump', jumping being the process and the jump being what is jumped; and we may speak of 'jumping a ditch,' jumping again being the process but the ditch being what is jumped. In these examples, the jump and the ditch are accusatives of the process jumping. Clearly, however, the jump is not independent of the jumping whereas the ditch is independent of the jumping. When the former kind of relationship obtains, the accusative is connate with the process; and when the latter kind of relationship obtains, the accusative is alien to the process. Now, when one has a sensation, the sensation is a connate accusative of the sensing; but when one describes the sensation, the sensation is an alien accusative to the describing.

Ayer correctly points out that "in allowing that the descriptions which people give of their experiences may be factually mistaken, we are dissociating having an experience from knowing that one has it. To know that one is having whatever experience it may be, one must not only have it but also be able to identify it correctly . . ." (72). It makes no sense to say of someone that he *knows* he is having an experience but does not know which one; and he does not know which one unless he can identify it, which is to say, describe it. But it does make sense to say that he is having an experience but does not know which one, that is, that he is having an experience but cannot describe it.

---

16 C. J. Ducasse, *Nature, Mind and Death,* 1951, pp. 253-254.

Thus, to return to the second leopard-experience, I may perfectly well experience the leopard's numerous spots without knowing how many spots there are. For the experience has a certain character, but is not itself an awareness of the character. To be sure, when I experience the leopard's spots, I experience forty-five spots. But to know that there are forty-five spots I must discover a one-to-one correspondence between the determinate numerousness of the spots and that of the positive integers up to and including 45. Merely experiencing the spots, then, is not itself a cognitive experience. The advocate of the incorrigibility thesis believes that experiencing the spots is somehow its own object, that is, that the experiencing is somehow an accusative of itself that therefore carries self-awareness with it. But he thereby admits that the experiencing has two distinct components, namely, the spots and the self-awareness, for the second component is identical with the self-awareness component of any other present experience. And if that is so, then unless the first components of the two experiences genuinely differ from each other, the two experiences would be qualitatively identical. Since no one, not even the advocate of the incorrigibility thesis, contends that all experiences are qualitatively identical, even he admits that the two components are distinct. But their being distinct means that in any given experience the two components are only contingently connected. Consequently, experiencing forty-five spots and being aware of or knowing that there are forty-five spots may not occur together. And if they do not, then I err when I reflect on, and accordingly report, my experience.

But how could such an error be detected? A report of an earlier present experience cannot be contradicted by a subsequent report of a now present experience. If line A looked slightly longer than line B, then a second look that now inclines me to say that the lines look the same length or that B looks slightly longer than A cannot now show that I was wrong. For the two reports do not conflict, since I do not make them simultaneously and their temporal scope is limited to the specious present of the relevant utterances or the specious present immediately preceding the relevant utterances. The past experience cannot be produced for reinspection, so no direct test of truth is possible. What this shows, however, is not that the relevant statements are incorrigible,

but that no single experience can justifiably compel us con-
clusively to reject any of them. And this is not the same as showing that there cannot be any ground on which to reject any of
them. For if having a certain sensation is identical with a particular person's being in a certain brain-state or undergoing a certain brain-process, then we can in principle correlate his first-
person reports of present experiences with his brain-states or
brain-processes during the specious present of the relevant utterances or immediately preceding the relevant utterances. We can
in principle have a universal statement 'Whenever C, then B', to
read 'Whenever this person has a certain sensation S, then a certain neurophysiological state obtains or a certain neurophysiological process occurs simultaneously with his reporting that he
has the sensation or immediately precedes his reporting that he
has it.' Then, if he reports that he has S, but B does not obtain or
occur at the appropriate time, we know that his report is incorrect.
And similarly for his reporting that he has other sensations.

Someone may object that this criterion of correctness for a
first-person report of present experience is implausible because
it entails that different brain-states or brain-processes occur for
each experience had, which seems far-fetched. But this feeling
of implausibility is a purely psychological matter, resting on our
ignorance of the brain itself and of the actual correlations between reports and brain-states and brain-processes. There is
nothing genuinely implausible about a finite number of experiences the having of each of which is identical with the existence or occurrence of one of a finite number of brain-states or
brain-processes.

But setting the alleged implausibility aside, someone may
object that the third-person statement 'He has sensation S' differs
from the first-person statement 'I have sensation S' in that the
former necessarily refers to a body whereas the latter does not.
The first-person report is complete if the sensation is described;
and it can be described without describing the person who has
it. Indeed, the first-person report should be understood as 'Sensation S now' or 'There is sensation S now' (the 'there is' being
understood in the sense of 'il y a' and 'es giebt' rather than in
that of 'voilà' and 'da ist'). Now, if the first-person report need
not refer to the speaker's body, surely the described sensation

cannot be identical with any of the states or processes of that body.

The reply to this objection is that, like an earlier objection, it confuses a sensation with having a sensation. It is not the former but the latter that is a term in the relevant identity, the other term being not a brain-state or brain-process but the body's being in a certain brain-state or its undergoing a certain brain-process. Thus, granting for argument's sake that a person can describe his present sensation without referring to his body, it does not follow that he can describe his having the sensation without referring to his body. And his having the sensation is what is relevant to the identity thesis.

Finally, someone may object that since my way of knowing (in whatever sense that term is appropriate here) that I have a sensation S differs from the way someone else knows that I am in a certain brain-state or undergoing a certain brain-process or from the way I myself should notice that state or witness that process, my having the sensation must differ from my being in the state or undergoing the process. In other words, if whatever I denote by my report that I have a sensation S is identical with whatever I or someone else denotes by the statement that I am in a certain brain-state or undergoing a certain brain-process, then it should be known by us the same way. And since it is not known by us the same way, the identity does not obtain.

This objection too is spurious. There is no reason why different people should be expected to know the same way that one of them is in a certain brain-state or undergoing a certain brain-process. Indeed, since they are different it is not at all odd that they do not. Thus, consider an ordinary process, namely, getting a haircut. If there is no mirror present, then although both the barber and I know that I am undergoing the process, we know it differently. For he knows it visually but I do not. Yet this does not warrant speaking of my undergoing two different processes. Similarly, there is no reason why there should not in principle be two ways to know I am having a sensation, one way available to me and the other to someone else. And as my inability to see my hair being cut is dependent upon the contingent absence of an appropriately situated mirror, so my inability to look into my brain is dependent upon the contingent absence of an appropriately administered local anaesthetic and appropriately situated visual aids. A patient under local anaesthetic sometimes watches surgery performed on him, and in principle I can similarly look into my skull and see that I am in a certain brain-state or undergoing a certain brain-process. The fact that we have not yet perfected the techniques that make this possible is parallel to the fact that at one time there was no mirror in which I could watch my own hair being cut.

The identity theory I have been advocating permits us to retain the belief that sensations are private, for the theory asserts that having a sensation is identical with a particular person's being in a brain-state or undergoing a brain-process. It permits us also to retain the belief that a first-person report of a present experience is not an avowal but a genuine factual statement that is true or false. And this theory provides a means of establishing the truth or falsity of that statement, to wit, by ascertaining whether or not the person is in the brain-state or undergoing the brain-process at the appropriate time. Given this identity theory, there is no inconsistency in speaking of an experiential language at least one of whose designative expressions does not denote any intersubjectively perceivable entity. Thus, the second concept of a private language is self-consistent.

The third concept of a private language is that of an experiential language none of whose designative expressions denotes any intersubjectively perceived entity. We found the second concept self-consistent because the occurrence of brain-states or brain-processes can be used to establish the truth or falsity of a first-person report of a present experience. The occurrence of such a state or process is not an intersubjectively perceivable entity, because it is not an entity at all. But to speak of such a state or process requires referring to some intersubjectively perceivable entity, namely, the body the occurrence of whose brain-states or brain-processes is the criterion for the truth of the relevant first-person report. But an intersubjectively perceivable entity may in fact not be perceived. Obviously, if there were in fact only one person in the world, then even if some of the designative expressions of his language denote intersubjectively perceivable entities, none of these entities could actually be perceived by more than one person. He would be in the situation of Robinson Crusoe before Man Friday arrived. Strictly speaking, of course, this last statement is not quite accurate. For we can distinguish someone who, like Robinson Crusoe, has already learned a language when he goes into isolation, from someone who has not. If the latter can invent and use a language, then the former, who has already learned one, clearly is able to use his language. I shall therefore examine the putative possibility of an isolated person's inventing and using a language despite his having no previous linguistic knowledge. If this is a genuine possibility there will be no need to examine the Robinson Crusoe situation separately.

To deny that the third concept of a private language is self-consistent is tantamount to asserting that it is logically impossible for a person isolated from others before he has become acquainted with a natural language to invent and to use a language in the continued absence of anyone else. The admittedly awkward expression "to invent and to use a language" suggests it might be possible for him to invent it but not to use it. I do not intend this suggestion. I employ the relevant expression only to emphasize that we are dealing not only with the possibility of a solitary someone's inventing a language without already knowing one but with that of a solitary someone's using an already known language.

We saw earlier that speaking a language involves conformity of one's speech acts to rules. We saw also that this does not mean that the conformative acts of making utterances are generally acts of following regulations stated antecedently to the utterances but acts instantiating a certain sort of regularity. Suppose, then, that an infant is abandoned on a desert island and somehow grows to adulthood in the absence of any other human being. It is certainly conceivable that his sensory apparatus be unimpaired and that like normally reared human beings he be able to sense and to recognize things on the island. The criterion for his being able to do so is his adjusting his behavior to them or adapting them to his use. Thus, if being bitten by a snake has caused him to become ill, he avoids the snake or snakes with similar markings or all snakes. Or if having a fire at night makes life more pleasant and he has learned that wood is combustible, he repeatedly gets wood, whether by gathering driftwood or by cutting down trees and drying them, and burns it. Unless he can recognize wood when he sees it and can remember that it is combustible and how to ignite it, he is not able to engage in the practice of making fires at night. Of course it is logically possible that his behavior is random, but then so would it be logically possible that actual instances of putative human recognition are random. I think it fair to say, therefore, that our imaginary island dweller recognizes things in the same sense of 'recognize' that we use when we speak of our recognizing things. He may begin by using names as proper names, but as his recognition broadens to include more things, the names become general names or class names. This is identical with the normally reared child's learning procedure, first learning to use 'dog', for instance, as the name of the animal by reference to which he is first acquainted with the word and gradually coming to use 'dog' as a common noun for that animal and relevantly similar animals. The island dweller first uses, for instance, the sound 'W' to refer to the particular piece of wood he burns, but gradually comes to use it for that piece and relevantly similar things. While he is burning it he may gather several other things and come to see that some are like the wood and some are not in respects other than being combustible, for instance, texture, color, hardness, brittleness, etc. The attempt to burn them is of course an additional test of similarity.

Here someone may deny that the learning procedures are the same and contend that the difference between them is crucial. He may point out that the normally reared child learns to use the sound 'dog' correctly by having his usage either approved or corrected by a native speaker, whereas the solitary island dweller does not have this check on his usage and so cannot distinguish between an instance of correctly using the sound 'W' and an instance of incorrectly using it, which means that he cannot learn a correct usage of 'W'. This seems to be the sort of thing Rhees has in mind when he writes:

> I cannot learn the color [red] unless I can see it, but I cannot learn it without language either. I know it because I know the language. . . . I can remember the color I saw. . . . But the identity—the sameness —comes from the language.

> . . . It might be said that I can know it is the same only if it
> [seems] the same; and that is something no language can tell me. . . .
> No language can tell me whether these two are the same color. . . .
> Without language I could not have told whether [they seem] the same,
> either; if only because I could not have asked.[17]

Although Rhees admits what is obvious, that no one can
ascertain by means of language alone that two things are the
same color, he goes further and asserts that without an existing
language there is no concept of sameness and so two colors cannot be said to be or to seem the same. But although to *say* that
two colors are the same requires that the speaker know a language that includes the word 'same' and know the correct usage
of that word, to *recognize* that two colors are the same does not
require him to know either. Suppose, for instance, I am expecting
a visitor whom I know I shall recognize when he appears although
I cannot adequately describe him in advance of his arrival. When
he does arrive, the confirmation that *he* is the expected person
lies in a bare perceptual recognition, not in my recognizing that
he answers to some description I have in advance. What I just
wrote may seem to contradict what I wrote earlier when discussing allegedly incorrigible first-person reports of present experience, for I wrote that it makes no sense to say that someone
knows he has an experience but not which experience. Do I now
say that someone knows he sees a certain person but does not
know that he sees that person? On the contrary, when he sees
the person, he knows he has an experience and that it is *seeing
that person*. But his knowledge does not consist in his being able
to *say* that the person whom he sees is the same as the person he
was expecting nor in his being able to *say* that the person whom
he sees satisfies a certain description. Indeed, his knowledge does
not consist in his being able to *say* anything whatever. It is a
serious error to believe that since recognition usually or always
is or can be expressed in words, it must be expressed in words.
And as with persons, so with colors.

Returning to our isolated island dweller, then, we may say
that he performs non-verbal acts of recognition. But how, it may
be asked, does he know whether or not he really recognizes some-

---

[17] R. Rhees, *op. cit.*, pp. 81-82.

thing? Well, how can anyone in an ordinary situation know he really recognizes something? By the subsequent occurrence of appropriate events, including other persons' performing speech acts affirming the correctness of the relevant recognition, such as 'Yes, you're right; that is red' or 'How nice of you to remember that I like wine with my meal.' But speech acts are not the only events that can be appropriate. In the colored-ball language game described earlier, bestowing a non-verbal reward is the sign of a correct color-recognition. Similarly, someone's savoring the wine served with the meal and eating with extraordinary gusto are events, or a complex event, that sanctions someone else's recognition that the *diner* is the person who likes wine with his meal, or that the diner is the person who likes *wine* with his meal, or that the diner is the person who likes wine *with his meal*, etc.

But here it may be objected that although it makes sense to speak of recognizing the color or the person, because whether or not it or he is recognized can be checked by the testimony of the native-speaking teacher or the diner, it does not make sense to speak of the isolated island dweller's recognizing anything, because his so-called check can be only another recollection. If, for instance, he wants to avoid snakes and believes that the creature before him is a snake, the only way he can check his putative recognition is either by again trying to recall whether or not the creature is a snake and so merely by making another memory report or by not avoiding the snake, again being bitten, and then recalling that being bitten is the sort of thing that happened when last he encountered a snake. But to check one memory-report by another memory-report is not really to check the first report at all. Indeed, Wittgenstein, whose objection this is, contends that the procedure is as if someone were to buy several copies of the morning paper to assure himself that what it said was true. "But justification consists in appealing to something independent."[18]

_____

[18] Ludwig Wittgenstein, *Philosophical Investigations*, Sec. 265. What Wittgenstein believed about this matter is not by any means clear. For compare: What is the criterion for the sameness of two images? . . . . For myself, when it is my image: nothing" (*Ibid.*, Sec. 377). "If I know [something] only from my own case, then I know what *I* call that, not what anyone else does" (*Ibid.*, Sec. 347).

What does 'independent' mean? In the proposed objection it obviously does not mean 'exclusive of the memory report being tested', for any other memory-report is independent of that one. And as Findlay suggests, there is no "fundamental difference between a standard of correctness depending upon the presence of a number of mutually confirming tendencies in *one and the same person*—all prompting him to use words in certain circumstances —and a standard of correctness depending on the very same tendencies when distributed among a *number of persons*."[19] This point is worth developing in detail. Wittgenstein writes that "justification by experience comes to an end [and that] if it did not it would not be justification."[20] But what is the "end" of which he writes? I submit that, whether he knew it or not, it is some bare recognition, such as I mentioned previously. The contention that the testimony of others is required to check a putative recognition is puzzling, because their testimony would have to be recognized as testimony and as the specific testimony it is. Suppose I see before me something I believe is a snake and should therefore be called 'S', which is the sign I publicly learned to use to denote any snake. Suppose further, that public testimony is the check by which I ascertain that 'S' is the correct public sign with which to denote the thing before me. This may mean either that other people will say "Yes, you're right; it is an S" or that they themselves will use 'S' to denote it. On the first alternative, I must understand that their utterance is a positive sanction, which I cannot do unless I recognize their sounds as constituting a positive sanction. On the second alternative, I must recognize the sound 'S' when they make it and the situation in which they make it. The situation includes its being made when prompted by the non-verbal stimulation of something of a certain sort, namely a snake, and by the verbal stimulation of the question "What is that?" But then, on the second alternative, which is more likely what the objector intends, I must recognize that things are of the same sort as previously encountered things, or each bit of public testimony will be unlinked with my past and will there-

---

[19] J. N. Findlay, "Review of Wittgenstein's *Philosophical Investigations*", (1955), reprinted in his *Language, Mind, and Value*, 1963, pp. 197-207, at 201-202.

[20] Ludwig Wittgenstein, *Philosophical Investigations*, Sec. 485.

fore be useless in teaching me to use 'S' or in checking my use of 'S'.

Suppose the critic grants that 'independent' does not mean 'exclusive of the memory-report being tested', but presses the criticism by arguing that my reply commits the fallacy of arguing that since it is not possible actually to check every identification, there can be an uncheckable identification. Anscombe correctly observes that it is fallacious to argue from 'It is possible that it is impossible actually to check every identification' to 'It is possible that there is some uncheckable identification.'[21] My reply is that the criticism misses my point. My point is not that there is some uncheckable identification, but that every identification must terminate in some bare recognition, which is taken as basic with respect to the identification. The acceptance of this recognition has the character of dogma, but only in practice. In principle it too may be checked. But the further checks would themselves terminate in bare recognitions that in turn would be taken as basic with respect to their revelant identifications, and so on *ad infinitum*. This kind of infinite regress is not a defect in my theory, because no attempt is made to *prove* any statement by reference to any of the recognition-statements. Rather, in practice I exhaust justification by experience and simply accept something as of a certain sort and as correctly denoted by a certain sign. In principle, however, I am prepared to continue justification by experience.

I have been discussing how someone knows he is using a designative expression correctly and have said that he knows by a bare recognition that can be justified by the subsequent occurrence of appropriate events, regardless of whether or not these events involve behavior by any other person and regardless of whether or not, if they do, the behavior is linguistic. But someone may object that I have not given any criterion of meaning for the word 'same' as used in the private language of our imaginary island dweller who invented his language without having

---

[21] G. E. M. Anscombe, *An Introduction to Wittgenstein's Tractatus*, 1958, pp. 138-139. She is criticizing A. J. Ayer's *The Problem of Knowledge* (pp. 63-64), which presents an argument similar to mine. His reply to her argument, in *The Concept of a Person*, 1963, p. 42, also is similar to mine.

had any previous linguistic experience. It will be alleged that, instead, I have explained why he makes a sound under certain conditions, but have used the word 'same' as it is used in our actual language, not in his language.

Of course I have used the word 'same' as it is used in our actual language. For my readers read *that* language and my explanation is addressed to my readers. Moreover, there is no reason to believe that the utterance 'same' cannot be used identically in both languages. What is meant by saying that the imaginary island dweller recognizes that a certain snake is of the same kind as a snake he saw previously is that if he had seen the two snakes simultaneously he would have said they were sufficiently alike to classify as of one kind. And what is meant by saying that he recognizes a certain snake as the same snake he saw previously is that if it were duplicated and he were to see both simultaneously he would say they were sufficiently alike to classify as identical except for position. What properties of things are selected to constitute a kind depends on the interests of the perceiver. And this is so in our ordinary public world and our ordinary natural languages.

If 'independent', in the statement that experiential justification of an identification consists in appealing to something independent, means 'exclusive merely of the memory-report on which the identification is immediately based', then it is clear that such independence is found in events occurring subsequently to the memory-report and in qualitatively distinct memory-reports. If, on the other hand, 'independent' there means 'utterly exclusive of memory', then it is equally clear that there cannot be either a private or a public language. For if I am to speak about anything, I must be able to refer to it in particular, to distinguish it linguistically from anything else. And I must be able to do this not merely when I first encounter it, but thereafter. But I cannot even refer to something in particular unless I can differentiate it by its sensory properties. And to do this only once is not enough for me to be able to speak about it, for to speak about it I must use language, and language, as we saw earlier, is rule-governed in the sense of being constituted by regularities of usage. But I cannot differentiate anything more than once unless I can recognize its sensory properties when I encounter them *after* first noticing them. And this recognition presupposes memory. Hence, if we explicate 'independent' one way, there can be both a private language of the third kind and a public language like any of our actual natural languages; but if we explicate it another way, there cannot be either.

Sometimes what seems to be behind a denial that a private language is possible is the belief that we cannot know another person as he knows himself. This belief manifests itself as the contention that there cannot be an experiential language some of whose expressions convey information to a non-user but not the same information as to the user. This concept of a private language is the fourth concept I have listed.

Suppose that the only person who speaks a certain language (not English), and who speaks only that language, explains the meaning of one of its perceptual expressions to a native speaker of English. Let the expression be 'guidilogog', and let me be the native speaker of English. Clearly he cannot explain its meaning by telling me in his language what it means, for I cannot understand his language. He can explain it to me ostensively, however, by pointing to something and saying 'guidilogog' either as he does so or upon seeing that my attention is focused on the thing to which he points. Let us assume that by this practice I come to understand that this thing is a guidilogog and am disposed to call it a guidilogog by using that expression to refer to it. Suppose that the thing is a dog. Clearly I cannot take the explanation to justify the statement that 'guidilogog' is synonymous with quadruped' or 'animal'. Suppose additional explanation by ostensive teaching gets me to understand that 'guidilogog' denotes any living animal or any living quadruped but that I am uncertain whether 'guidilogog' is synonymous with 'living animal' or 'living quadruped'. Surely the expression 'guidilogog' then conveys information both to the user of the private language and to me, but that information differs.

Here someone may object that I have established the self-consistency of this kind of private language by improperly construing the expression 'experiential language' in the definition so broadly as to include a perceptual expression. 'Experiential' is rather to be understood as restricting the relevant expressions to the kind of which the English expressions 'pain' and 'dislike' are instances.

But this objection is not serious, for the same thing can be done with whatever expression in the private language is synonymous with 'pain', say, 'jubet'. To be sure, 'jubet' cannot be taught to me ostensively by the person's pointing to a pain, but sentences in which 'jubet' occurs may be uttered by him in circumstances in which native speakers of English utter sentences in which 'pain' occurs. Let us suppose that he utters just enough sentences in which 'jubet' occurs so that I understand that 'jubet' is synonymous with 'pain' or 'distaste' without knowing with which. Here, as formerly with 'guidilogog', 'jubet' conveys information both to the user of the private language and to me, but the information differs.

The point of both examples is that the explanations of the meaning of a private-language expression may get me to understand the meaning to the extent of knowing some of its extension without as a matter of fact permitting me to understand its full extension or its intension.

It may yet be that this argument about partial translatability does not persuade someone who contends there cannot be a private language of the fourth kind. He may believe that the argument applies to a perceptual expression but not to a non-perceptual experiental expression. He may grant that 'jubet' is used in just those situations in which native speakers of English use 'pain', but may deny that 'pain' itself is meaningful. His reasoning is roughly this. Allegedly, 'pain' is a word used to denote something other than behavior, something known only to the person whose pain it is. This person allegedly learns what 'pain' means by having a pain, exhibiting certain behavior that is taken by other people as its natural expression in the circumstances in which it is exhibited, and being told by them that the behavior is caused by or concomitant with the pain. He does not learn it in the sense that he thereafter knows that he has a pain by inferring this fact from his self-observed behavior, but in the sense that he knows the name of a distinguishable phenomenon occurring in certain circumstances and of similar phenomena occurring in similar circumstances and uses the word 'pain' to denote the relevantly similar phenomena when they occur thereafter. But there cannot be a criterion for a correct identification of a pain, so it makes no sense to speak of a correct or an incorrect use of the word 'pain'.

First, as has already been shown, it does make sense to speak of correctly identifying something by relying on one's own behavior and memory. Second, not every expression of the form 'I have a . . .' is one for which it is appropriate to state that the noun that completes the expression denotes a thing. For instance, when I say 'I have a pair of mittens' I thereby refer to but two things I have, namely a left mitten and a right mitten, not to these two and a pair. Similarly, when I say 'I have a pain in my right arm' I thereby refer to but one thing I have, namely my right arm, not to my right arm and a pain. Now, I can have a language whose vocabulary is identical with English vocabulary except for the absence of 'pair' and 'pain' and whose syntactical rules differ slightly from those of English. In this language the expression 'two mittens paired' corresponds to the expression 'a pair of mittens' in actual English, and the expression 'my right arm hurts' corresponds to the expression 'I have a pain in my right arm' in actual English. Users of the modified English, unlike users of actual English, are not misled by the grammatical forms of these expressions into believing that there is anything over and above the mittens or the right arm in the situations in which they are mentioned in the relevant expressions. Thus, although the statement 'I have a pain in my right arm' is a genuine report, it is a report that I have a certain brain-state or am undergoing a certain brain-process that is nomologically associated with a certain localization of pain.

After erroneously denying that there can be a check for a first-person pain statement, Wittgenstein infers that uttering the expression 'I am in pain' or 'I have a pain' is part of pain-behavior itself, that it is learned behavior that replaces the natural expression of pain. His argument is rather interesting, because although psychologically persuasive, it is utterly fallacious.

> Suppose everyone had a box with something in it: we call it a "beetle". No one can look into anyone else's box, and everyone says he knows what a beetle is only by looking at *his* beetle.—Here it would be quite possible for everyone to have something different in his box. One might even imagine such a thing constantly changing.—But suppose the word

"beetle" had a use in these people's language? If so it would not be used as the name of a thing. The thing in the box has no place in the language-game at all; not even as a *something*: for the box might even be empty.—No, one can 'divide through' by the thing in the box; it cancels out, whatever it is.

That is to say: if we construe the grammar of the expression of sensation on the model of 'object and designation' the object drops out of consideration as irrelevant.[22]

In the case of pain *I* believe that I can give myself a private exhibition [of it]. . . . But for the private exhibition you don't have to give yourself actual pain; it is enough to *imagine* it—for instance, you screw up your face a bit. And do you know what you are giving yourself this exhibition of is pain and not, for example, a facial expression? And how do you know what you are to give yourself an exhibition of before you do it? This *private* exhibition is an illusion.[23]

How does a human being learn the meaning of . . .the word "pain" for example. Here is one possibility: words are connected with the primitive, the natural, expressions of the sensation and used in their place. A child has hurt himself and he cries; and then adults talk to him and teach him exclamations and, later, sentences. They teach the child new pain-behavior.

"So you are saying that the word 'pain' really means crying—On the contrary: the verbal expression of pain replaces crying and does not describe it.[24]

One can agree that in screwing up one's face he is not giving himself a private exhibition of pain and yet not infer therefrom that the pain is nothing distinct from the behavior. Wittgenstein's beetle fantasy misconceives the alleged relation between pain and pain-behavior.[25] Neither his beetle nor his box is alleged to be a natural expression of the other, and so it makes perfectly good sense to say there is a box that has no beetle in it. But Wittgenstein accepts enough of the traditional view of pain to render this argument defective. He accepts that pain and instinctive

---

[22] Ludwig Wittgenstein, *Philosophical Investigations*, Sec. 293.

[23] *Ibid.*, Sec. 311.

[24] *Ibid.*, Sec. 244.

[25] But cf. George Pitcher, *The Philosophy of Wittgenstein*, 1964, p. 298: "The analogy with pain is perfectly clear. If 'pain' is supposed to denote a somewhat (including a nothing) which each person can observe only in his own case, then the somewhat "cancels out"; and if the sole function of the word 'pain' is to denote it, the word is at once deprived of any use."

pain-behavior are nomologically connected, the latter being the "natural expression" of the former. Hence, the fact that we cannot imagine a pain occurring apart from its expression does not entail that the pain is not something distinct from its expression and that accordingly it cannot be referred to independently of referring to its expression. Concomitants, though not separate, are yet distinct.

Moreover, one should not argue, as Pitcher does, that Wittgenstein is denying only "a thesis about language, namely that the word 'pain' names or designates [something] that the person feels, in a way which is even remotely like the way that the words for publicly observable things name or designate them" and not "that when a person is in pain, he very often and perhaps always feels something. . . ."[26] Wittgenstein is denying the factual thesis too. For if the word 'pain' cannot sensibly be used to name or designate anything, then it makes no sense to speak designatively of my pain or your pain. Nor does it make sense to speak of the "something" I have, which 'pain' cannot be used to designate, for 'something' belongs "to our common language" and so according to Wittgenstein cannot be used to designate a pain if a pain is conceived as his beetle fantasy conceives it (see *Philosophical Investigations*, Sec. 261). Of course I do not deny that 'I am in pain' is sometimes used as a substitute for the speaker's natural expression of pain. Clearly it is, but only sometimes.

To return briefly to the beetle fantasy. Wittgenstein says that no one can look into anyone else's box, but if he had added that the outside of each beetle box not only is observable but exhibits characteristic marks of having a beetle in it, then provided someone could learn what these marks are on his own box there is no unique problem of introducing 'beetle' into the language. I may see, for instance, that my box moves only when the beetle in it moves against one of its sides. If I can find no external cause of the movement of someone else's box, I shall say that he has a beetle in his box and that the beetle's moving against one of the sides of his box causes the box to move. When I say he has a beetle in his box I may of course be mistaken. But I am not guilty of any conceptual absurdity.

---

[26] *Ibid.*, p. 298.

Whatever we make of Wittgenstein's beetle fantasy, my argument about partial translatability shows that some of the expressions of an experiential language do convey different information to a user from the information it conveys to a non-user. Hence the fourth kind of private language is self-consistent. But it may be said that although such a private language is possible, it remains to be shown that a similar private language none of whose expressions can convey the same information to the user as to the non-user is also possible.

The argument about partial translatability shows that explanations by ostensive teaching can teach me some of the extension of the expression whose meaning is being explained and yet not permit me to understand its full extension. I shall now argue that it is impossible by this method of explanation to teach me the intension of the expression and that therefore a private language of the fifth sort is self-consistent. For since I cannot learn the intension of even one expression of the putatively private language, none of its expressions can convey the same information to me as to the user.

Suppose I know the full extension of 'guidilogog'. There is not just one intension that is compatible with this extension, so ascertaining the intension is not a matter of logical deduction from the extension but a matter of choice between numerous properties within the given extension. But even this will not do, because for any designative expression whose extension is known, all logically possible entities that can be, as well as actually are, denoted by it must be considered for me to be able to ascertain its intension. But the logically possible entities that can be denoted by it are infinite, so it is impossible to ascertain the intension of an expression by observing how it is actually used. Since the user of the private language knows only his language and I know only English, he cannot explicitly state that 'guidilogog' is synonymous with a certain English expression. And so 'guidilogog', whose intension he knows, means one thing to him and another to me.

A simple example of a situation like that just discussed in the abstract is in order. Suppose the intension of 'human' is 'featherless biped whose relative brain weight is between x and y', 'x' and 'y' being finite decimals. Suppose further that two non-English-

speaking linguists investigating English agree that the extension
of 'human' includes only featherless bipeds but that one linguist
contends its intension is 'featherless biped' whereas the other contends its intension is 'featherless biped whose relative brain
weight is between x and y'. Depending on what native speakers
of English are willing to predicate 'human' of, different conclusions about its intension are warranted. Thus, if native speakers
are willing to predicate 'human' only of featherless bipeds each
of whose relative brain weights is between x and y, then the intension of 'human' is not merely 'featherless biped' but 'featherless biped whose relative brain weight is between x and y'. But
there are infinitely many possible values of 'x' and 'y' and the
linguists cannot learn their actual values merely by knowing the
relative brain weights of *some* actual and possible featherless
bipeds to which native speakers apply or are willing to apply the
term 'human'. The linguists may know the relative brain weights
of all actual featherless bipeds, but since there is an infinity of
possible featherless bipeds, each having a different relative brain
weight, they cannot exhaust the possible values of 'x' and 'y' by
questioning native speakers about whether or not they are willing
to apply 'human' to featherless bipeds whose relative brain
weights are such-and-such or so-and-so. Accordingly, they cannot ascertain the intension of 'human' by observing how native
speakers of English use it. Hence, although it conveys information to native speakers and to the non-native speaking linguists,
the information necessarily cannot be *known* to be the same.

We come at last to the sixth concept of a private language,
namely, an experiential language none of whose expressions can
be understood by a non-user. Such a "language" is not, as Ayer
thinks, one that "is used by some particular person to refer only
to his own private experiences",[27] but as Malcolm states, one that
"cannot be understood by anyone other than the speaker".[28] Very
little argument is needed to show that this concept is not self-
consistent. I have already explained that language is rule-governed in the sense that it consists of a system of dispositions to
perform certain speech acts under certain specifiable conditions.

27 A. J. Ayer, "Can There Be a Private Language?", *Belief and Will*, Aristotelian Society Supplementary Volume XXVIII, 1954, p. 64.
28 Norman Malcolm, *Knowledge and Certainty*, 1963, p. 97.

But a putative language that no one other than its user can understand even in principle must be one without rules, for if it has rules, then there is no reason why another human being cannot in principle learn those rules and so understand the language. But the concept of a language without rules is self-contradictory.

None of the other concepts of a private language has as a necessary condition that no one but the user be able to understand it even in principle. And this condition is so radical that it strips the putative language of rules. Accordingly, for the putative user of this language there could be no criterion of correct usage, not the features of the external world nor his own recollections. If there were a criterion of correct usage, it would determine a rule of usage. And since this putative language has no rules, there is no way of knowing what sounds to produce in what circumstances. Under this condition, speaking a language is out of the question: there are no words, but only sounds such as the wind may cause as it passes through the leaves of a tree.

I have shown that the statement that there cannot be a private language is ambiguous because there are six concepts of a private language. Of these, only one is inconsistent. That one, however, is irrelevant to the non-solipsism argument based on the alleged necessity of a linguistic community if there is to be a language. Hence, it is fruitless to argue that because a private language is impossible, there must be at least two persons, each independent of the other's will, or in other words, that because a private language is impossible, solipsism is false.

CHAPTER III

Solipsism

> "Why you're only a sort of thing in his dream!" [said Tweedledee.]
> "If that there King was to wake," added Tweedledum, "you'd go out—bang!—just like a candle!"
> —LEWIS CARROLL, *Through the Looking-Glass*

> A thousand see the nonsensicalness of a statement without being able to disprove it formally.
> —GEORGE CHRISTOPH LICHTENBERG, *Aphorisms*

Since the private-language inquiry does not exclude solipsism, I now examine that doctrine on its own. Whiteley states solipsism to be "the doctrine that the only person existing in the universe is myself."[1] I believe that this doctrine is *not* identical with solipsism, but merely with scepticism about the possibilty of knowledge of other minds.[2] Notice that Whiteley's version of solipsism is compatible with there being putative other-persons whose appearances and reactions are entirely independent of my control and who may be taken as independently existing objects about which I may sensibly ask whether or not they have experiences like those I have. Indeed, by speaking of "the world" and "the universe" as he does, Whiteley presupposes that there is a world and a universe *in which* I exist. This contention is incompatible with solipsism conceived as the doctrine that I alone subsist and everything else exists only as my conceptual or perceptual

---

[1] C. H. Whiteley, *An Introduction to Metaphysics*, 1955, p. 95.
[2] I discuss this scepticism in Chapter Five.

construction. This second account of solipsism is the true account
and the one, therefore, that presents the perceptual issue of how
to justify belief in the existence of a world independent of my
existence. Notice, however, that this perceptual issue is not how
to distinguish delusive perceptual experience from veridical perceptual experience, for in presupposing that there is veridical
perceptual experience, that issue presupposes that there *is* an independent perceptual reality to be perceived or that the question
how to distinguish the two sorts of experience arises *within* the
solipsist's non-independent perceptual reality. In either event, the
issue differs from the solipsist issue, which is whether or not I
alone subsist, everything else being only my conceptual or perceptual construction.

Whether or not solipsism is true is sometimes believed to turn
on the question whether or not any physical object can continue
to exist when unperceived and unthought of by the putative
solipsist. This question is vague, however, for the phrase "can
continue to exist" is puzzling.[3] What is it for a physical object not
to continue to exist? Suppose a piece of chinaware is struck full
force with a sledge hammer. Thereafter, does the piece of chinaware no longer exist, but instead pieces of porcelain? This would
be a linguistically deviant way to describe the change. Rather, the
piece of chinaware has been shattered beyond repair. Similarly,
physical objects of other kinds can be broken, burned, rent, and
razed, etc. But, *if* an object can exist unperceived and unthought
of, it can be thus destroyed when neither perceived nor thought
of by any person. Vibration of a shelf may cause a piece of chinaware to fall from it and shatter into small pieces, or faulty electrical wiring may cause a fire that burns a book to ashes, or wind
may rend a sail to shreds, or a storm may raze a house, etc.—all
while no one perceives or thinks of the destroyed object. Clearly,
the solipsist cannot contend that if an object is unperceived and
unthought of, it cannot then be destroyed. For he denies that any
unperceived and unthought of object can exist. Nor can he mean
by an object's ceasing to exist when unperceived and unthought
of that the object disappears the moment no one perceives or

---

[3] Cf. Leonard Linsky, "On Ceasing to Exist", *Mind*, LXIX, No. 274, pp. 249-
250 (1960).

thinks of it, since for an object to disappear is for it to be in some *place* other than that in which we initially expect it and those in which we subsequently seek it. And to be at a place, any place, entails that there is a place to be at. The solipsist, however, denies that any place can exist unperceived and unthought of. For if it could exist unperceived and unthought of, then either it would be *per impossible,* some sort of physical receptacle to be filled (like a wastepaper basket), or it would be something defined relationally by the relative position of the object occupying it. If the latter alternative, then the object occupying it would itself, *per impossible,* exist unperceived and unthought of. For if it were perceived or thought of, so could the place it occupies and thereby defines be perceived or thought of.

I think there is no clear model for 'ceases to exist' in this context and that what is meant by the contention that no physical object can continue to exist when unperceived and unthought of is this. If a physical object exists, then someone perceives or thinks of it. And if at any time that object ceases to be perceived and to be thought of, then necessarily it no longer exists. In short, the existence of every physical object allegedly depends on its being perceived or thought of. The contention, accordingly, is curious indeed, for it is not clear whether the necessity is a logical necessity or a contingent necessity. If it is a logical necessity, then the contention is tantamount to a stipulation how to use the expression 'physical object' in certain contexts. And since the stipulation recommends a usage radically different from that accorded to the expression by the conventions of our actual language, it needs to be justified. If the necessity is contingent, then there should be some empirical method by which to establish that the contention is true or that it is false. But there is no way this can be done directly, the impossibility owing to the fact that for anyone directly to ascertain of any physical object either that it does continue to exist when neither perceived nor thought of or that it does not entails that he perceive or think of it. Nor can it be done indirectly, since for anyone indirectly to ascertain of any physical object either that it does continue to exist when neither perceived nor thought of or that it does not entails that he rely on testimony by someone who does perceive or think of the object while the first person does not.

Can I, *qua* solipsist, rely on the evidence of someone else's testimony? No. Because if this someone else is, as solipsism states, a perceptual or conceptual construction of mine, then his testimony also is a perceptual or conceptual construction of mine. And whatever testimony I construct, being my construction, depends only on me and not on anything independent of me. The solipsism issue, then, turns on the concept of something *independent* of me. As Wittgenstein remarks, "The world is independent of my will."[4] Independent how? In that "I cannot bend the happenings of the world to my will: I am completely powerless."[5]

An obvious objection to the quest for something independent of me is that whatever I assert to be independent of me is merely what *I take to be* independent of me. The allegedly independent world, it is objected, owes its so-called independence merely to my believing that a certain perceptual construct of mine is independent of me. And if this is so, then the allegedly independent world is not independent of me at all. But this objection is spurious, for in allowing the distinction between an independent world and one that I merely believe to be independent, the objection admits the meaningfulness of the concept of an independent world and thereby reduces the objector's scepticism from doubt of its very meaningfulness to doubt that it is exemplified.

Let us therefore examine the suggestion that there is something independent of me. Of the many bodies that occupy my perceptual space, can I distinguish one that alone is mine? If so, that one is *not* independent of me, whereas the others are. According to Strawson,[6]

> for each person there is one body which occupies a certain causal position in relation to that person's perceptual experience, a causal position which in various ways is unique in relation to each of the various kinds of perceptual experience he has; and—as a further consequence—that this body is also unique for him as an *object* of the various kinds of perceptual experience which he has. (92)

Strawson contends that the facts described in general by saying that my body occupies a special place in my experiences explains

---

[4] Ludwig Wittgenstein, *Tractatus Logico-Philosophicus,* 1921, 6.373.
[5] Ludwig Wittgenstein, *Notebooks 1914-1916,* 1961, p. 73.
[6] P. F. Strawson, *Individuals,* 1959.

"why I feel peculiarly attached to what in fact I call my own body; they even might be said to explain why, granted that I am going to speak of one body as *mine*, I should speak of *this* body as mine" (93). What are the facts of perceptual experience Strawson has in mind? Take visual experience, for instance. He writes:

> First, there is that group of empirical facts of which the most familiar is that if the eyelids of that body are closed, the person sees nothing. To this group belong all the facts known to ophthalmic surgeons. Second, there is the fact that what falls within his field of vision at any moment depends in part on the *orientation* of his eyes, i.e., on the direction his head is turned in, and on the *orientation* of his eyeballs in their sockets. And, third, there is the fact that *where he sees from*— or what his possible field of vision at any moment is—depends on where his body, and in particular his head, is located. (90)

Strawson emphasizes that it is only a contingent fact that, for any person, these three kinds of dependence involve the same body. Thus, for a subject of visual experience, S, and two bodies, A and B, it may be that S has visual experiences if and only if A's eyes are open and irrespective of whether or not B's eyes are open, and that S's field of vision depends on where B is but not on where A is. It is clear from this example that there cannot be any single purely visual experience, no matter of what sort, whose occurrence is the criterion by which a person ascertains that a certain body is his own. Perhaps, however, that experiences of all three kinds of dependence involve the same body is the criterion by which he ascertains that a certain body is his own. Suppose, for instance, for a subject of visual experiences, S, and bodies B_1 B_2, . . . B_n (where 'n' is some positive integer), that S has a visual experience if and only if B_1's eyes are open and irrespective of whether or not any other body's eyes are open, that what falls within S's field of vision at any moment depends partly on the orientation of B_1's eyes and eyeballs and not on the orientation of those of any other body, and that S's possible field of vision at any moment depends on where B_1's non-severed head is located but not on where any other body's head is located. Given these facts, is S justified in concluding that B_1 is his body? I think not. Call B_1 his putative physical body and then consider the possibility of an out-of-the-body experience.[7] A person sometimes has what appears to him at the time he has them to be ordinary visual experiences of actual things and persons (including his own physical body), from a point of view located in what he then takes to be the ordinary space-time continuum but outside his physical body. On these occasions the person generally appears to have a secondary body that closely resembles his putative physical body in shape, size, and outward appearance, but is much more plastic and less ponderable. Furthermore, on these occasions the person's main consciousness seems to be centered in the secondary body, in the sense in which it ordinarily is felt to be centered in his putative physical body. The person ostensibly sees his own putative physical body as it would normally be seen by a putative other-person whose physical body were situated where the secondary body is situated; and he does not see his own putative physical body as if he were situated where it is. He also sees other things from the point of view determined by the position occupied by his secondary body and not by his putative physical body. Thus, on these occasions the three kinds of dependence related to visual experience are exemplified by a body that the person does *not* take to his own physical body. That this is so is clear from the following partial account of an out-of-the-body experience.

> . . . he began to have visual experiences. He ostensibly *saw* his bed a few feet *below* him, and *felt* his body as floating rigid and horizontal above it. Gradually he got a clearer and clearer sight of the room and its contents as from that point of view. . . . He states that so far he had taken for granted that it was his *ordinary physical body* that was concerned in all this. . . .
>
> When he took himself to be about six feet above the bed, he found himself *turned* from floating horizontally to standing upright on the floor, still in the cataleptiform state. Next he became free to move

---

[7] Full descriptions and a detailed discussion of such experiences are found in C. D. Broad, *Lectures on psychical Research*, 1962, Chapter VI and *passim*. See also Oliver Fox, *Astral Projection*, 1962. I know that someone may object that the descriptions of these experiences are unintelligible. I too suspect them of unintelligibility. But I prefer to use them nevertheless. I find this issue puzzling, but tangential to my immediate concern.

at will, and he turned round and faced the bed. He then, for the first time, ostensibly saw his physical body lying on the bed, and noted that he was viewing it and the other contents of the room from a point of view external to his physical body and located within another body, which I will call (without thereby committing myself to any view as to the objective facts at the back of these experiences) his 'secondary body.'[8]

It follows that even the joint satisfaction, by the same body, of a dependence-condition of each kind cannot be the criterion by which a person ascertains that that body is his own.

A clue to a different criterion from the one just rejected is found in a sentence in Broad's account of the aforementioned out-of-the-body experience. He writes of the experient that "all his senses, except that of *touch*, seemed to be working normally" (184). Now, a person who is ostensibly visually perceiving certain objects may walk up to them and make bodily movements appropriate to touching them. If he does not thereupon get the tactual sensations correlated in the usual way with the details of his ostensible visual perception, the veridicality of that perception is *pro tanto* invalidated. This perfectly acceptable criterion of perceptual delusiveness has an interesting consequence when applied to an out-of-the-body experience. In such an experience, apparently all the objects seen from the point of view of the secondary body, including parts of that body itself, are non-tactual. But in ordinary perceptual situations a body has touch sensitivity, and even if no other visible object is tactual, at least it is. In ordinary circumstances kinaesthetic sensations associated with bringing one of my index fingers to my forehead and then pressing the former against the latter result in two pressure sensations of which I am directly aware, an index-finger-tip-pressure and a forehead-pressure. And similarly for any other part of my body to which I press my index finger. However, if in ordinary circumstances I press one of my index fingers to any part of any body other than the one I commonsensically take to be mine, only one pressure sensation results of which I am directly aware, namely, an index-finger-tip-pressure. Direct awareness of pressure sensations is my criterion for accepting the loci of sensation as parts

---

[8] C. D. Broad, *op. cit.*, p. 184.

of my body. The whole of my body is the set of contiguous places of whose pressure sensations I can be directly aware, plus the set of contiguous places falling within the volume determined by the surface so specified, plus certain specifiable contiguous places external to that surface, e.g. hair and nails. Now, if I have an out-of-the-body experience during which my main consciousness seems to be centered in my secondary body, movement of my secondary body does not result in any pressure sensation of which I am directly aware. Hence, my secondary body is not the body that is identical with *my* body, although it is somehow intimately connected with my body. Of course, during the duration of the out-of-the-body experience, my non-secondary body is not actually having any tactual sensations of which I am directly aware. But the important point is that it, unlike my secondary body, is not making bodily movements appropriate to my having certain tactual sensations correlated in the usual way with my ostensible visual perception. Thus, what I have here is an invalidating rule that excludes as other-than-mine certain bodies that, but for the application of the rule, I should consider candidates for being mine.

I conclude, then, that of all bodies in my perpetual space, exactly one is central to that space, in the sense that I *veridically* perceive objects as from a center located within that body but not as from a center located in any other body. And this perceptually central body is my body. Notice that its centrality is determined by veridical perception not by ostensible perception, for if I were to have a certain kind of out-of-the-body experience my secondary body would be perceptually central insofar as ostensible perception is concerned.

Of course, the question now arises, 'Since when I am having such an out-of-the-body experience I have no veridical perception but only ostensible perception, does it follow that I am then somehow disembodied?' It does not. My perceptual experience is determined by modification in my brain, my brain being the brain in the body that is central to my veridical perception; and my being in a certain brain-state or undergoing a certain brain-process is identical with my having a certain experience.[9]

---

[9] This theory is discussed in detail in Chapter Two, pp. 56-57 and Chapter Four, pp. 104-113.

Surely nothing about out-of-the-body experiences is more puzzling epistemologically than ordinary gross hallucinations, although the latter are admittedly far more numerous than the former.

The search for something independent of me has ended with the discovery of a criterion of determining which body is my physical body. I emphasize that the discovery is of the *criterion*, not of which body is my physical body. There is an important sense in which I cannot but know which body is my physical body, even though I may be unable to give a correct analysis of what I mean by saying that it is mine. For it is an analytic truth that my veridical perceptual experience cannot be anyone else's, though someone else can have veridical perceptual experiences that are qualitatively identical to mine. And since my veridical perceptual experiences *invariably* are centered in a particular body, I take that body to be my physical body. What I may not realize if I am unable to give a correct analysis of what I mean by saying that it is mine is that the invariability is logically necessary. To be sure, that my veridical perceptual experiences belong to the particular body to which they do is only contingently true. But this means not that they might belong to another body but that the body to which they do belong need not exist and so neither need they exist. But given that these experiences do exist, their belonging to the body they do is logically necessary.

Earlier in my discussion, I suggested that the solipsism issue turns on the concept of something independent of me and that the independence is explicable in relation to my will. I shall now clarify that suggestion. My beliefs about my perceptual space and its occupants carry with them a system of habit that presents various possibilities of action to me. The beliefs are assimilated to, or intend, these possibilities of action and thereby the action itself. Now, any attempt to act is something I make at will; and any action I successfully perform is something I do at will. But in even the most favorable circumstances, there is exactly one body whose movements I appropriately control so as to act. The action I perform, by definition, is intended and so involves a meaningful felt continuity of belief-action, possibility-action, and performance. As Hampshire points out, insofar as I am acting, my action itself is "governed by an intention that enters into the action and that differentiates it from mere physical movement."[10] My body is that which, as Wittgenstein puts it, I bend to my will, whereas the world is that which I cannot bend to my will.

I emphasized above that although I formulate a criterion determining which body is my physical body, I do not *discover* which body is my physical body by using that criterion. Without ever applying the criterion, I know which body is mine. Indeed, there is something absurd about my inquiring, in ordinary circumstances, which body is mine, as though I can somehow point to an object and ask whether or not it is my physical body. For it makes no sense to speak of my experiences as existing independently of the particular body to which they belong. I am not something independent of that body, something that has experiences one of which is an experience of "owning" or "belonging to" that body. Of course it makes perfectly good sense for me to inquire whether or not something to which I point is *part* of my body, for a particular part of my body can be removed from the rest of it. But I attach no sense to the statement that *all* my body can be removed from me.

It sometimes has been held that solipsism can be expressed without the solipsist's using any personal pronoun. Thus, if I am the solipsist, I have only to describe and to enumerate my experiences without calling them mine and to assert that there is nothing other than these experiences. 'I' can be defined as 'the set of experiences to which this (experience) belongs'. 'This' identifies a particular experience in the set, such that the experience is simultaneous with the specious present in which 'this' is uttered. The experience can be further specified by describing its content with such words as 'here' and 'there', which are directional proper names, and 'green', 'high-pitched', 'damp', 'acrid', and 'bitter', etc., which are sense-category descriptives. The ordinary English sentence, 'I see a green ball', for instance, is equivalent to 'There is a green ball'.

This way of putting the solipsist thesis makes it quite plain that the so-called *self* is not part of the world but is its limit. Solipsism coincides with realism: "The self of solipsism shrinks

---

[10] Stuart Hampshire, *Thought and Action*, 1960, pp. 74-75. Cf. A. I. Melden, *Free Action*, 1961, pp. 194ff. and *passim*.

to a point without extension, and there remains the reality co-
ordinated with it."[11] Solipsism as a true doctrine comes to no
more than this: if I want to talk about the universe without
talking as if it is independent of me, I can do so by talking without mentioning myself; for if I never mention myself explicitly
or implicitly, the concept of something independent of *me* makes
no sense. In short, insofar as solipsism is true, it is trivial; and
insofar as it is not trivial, it is not true.

---

[11] Ludwig Wittgenstein, *Tractatus Logico-Philosophicus,* 1921, 5.64. See
also 5.631 and 5.632.

The Identity Theory

Roughly speaking, to say of *two* things that they are identical
is nonsense, and to say of *one* thing that it is identical with
itself is to say nothing at all.
—LUDWIG WITTGENSTEIN, *Tractatus Logico-Philosophicus*

(One of the most difficult of the philosopher's tasks is to
find out where the shoe pinches.)
—LUDWIG WITTGENSTEIN, *Notebooks 1914-1916*

In this chapter I analyze and justify a reductive materialistic
conception of mind.[1] I begin by examining a theory according
to which someone's mental events or experiences are identical
with certain events or processes in his brain. There is a sufficiently formidable objection to this theory to warrant rejecting it.
I therefore defend a second theory, according to which someone's having an experience is identical with his being in a certain
brain-state or undergoing a certain brain-process, i.e., his brain's
being in a certain state or undergoing a certain change. I have
already discussed these theories briefly in Chapter Two, and
arguments stated there are reintroduced at appropriate points
in this chapter.

My materialism states that the only entities existing in the

---

[1] My theory derives from the work of J. J. C. Smart, especially his "Sensations and Brain Processes", *The Philosophical Review*, LXVIII, 2 (1959), pp.
141-156 and his *Philosophy and Scientific Realism*, 1963.

world are atoms and ensembles of atoms, that the only properties
are those of the atoms and the ensembles, and that the only rela-
tions are those that obtain between atoms, between atoms and
ensembles, and between ensembles of atoms. Accordingly, human
beings are ensembles of atoms. But human beings have experiences: sensations, feelings, thoughts, moods, attitudes, expecta-
tions, etc. One materialistic conception of mind states that
experiences or mental states or states of consciousness can be
accounted for materialistically, that mental phenomena can properly be regarded as distinct brain-states or brain-processes of the
person whose experiences they are.

What sort of identity does this theory assert to obtain between a person's experiences or states of consciousness and his
brain-states or brain-processes? First, the contention is *not* that
there is a one-to-one correlation between experiences and brain-
states or brain-processes. There can be such a correlation only if
there are *two* things, for it makes no sense to speak of correlating
something with itself. But the theory states that there are not
two things, but only one. It states that the experience or state
of consciousness and the brain-state or brain-process are the same
thing in the sense that the substantive expression used to designate the experience or state of consciousness and the substantive
expression used to designate the brain-state or brain-process have
the same extension. Second, the contention is *not* that statements
about experiences can be translated without remainder into statements about brain-states or brain-processes. The relevant identity is not an identity of meaning, but a factual identity. A statement reporting that I am having a certain experience is not being
said to have the same meaning or the same logical grammar as
one reporting that I am in a certain brain-state or undergoing a
certain brain-process. But insofar as each statement refers to
something, it refers to the same thing, to wit, a brain-state or
brain-process.

Smart calls the kind of identity he has in mind "strict identity"
and explicates it by example.[2] (1) Seven is strictly identical with
the smallest prime number greater than Five. (2) A flash of
lightning is strictly identical with an electrical discharge to the

---

    [2] J. J. C. Smart, "Sensations and Brain Processes", pp. 145-148.

earth from a cloud of ionized water-molecules. (3) He points out that when he says that a certain successful general is the same as a certain small boy who stole certain apples, he is not saying that the general and the boy are strictly identical but only that the successful general he sees before him is "a time slice of the same four-dimensional object of which the small boy stealing apples is an earlier time slice",[3] whereas he is saying that the four-dimensional object that has the general-he-sees-before-him for its late time slice is strictly identical with the four-dimensional object that has the small-boy-stealing-apples for an early time slice. (4) He vacillates about whether or not the Morning Star is strictly identical with the Evening Star, because someone may object that the Morning Star is only spatiotemporally continuous with the Evening Star.

The first thing to notice about these examples is that three of them are instances of contingent identity and one of them is an instance of logically necessary identity. This in itself is puzzling, for Smart contends that the identity that allegedly obtains between an experience and a brain-state or brain-process is a contingent identity. The identity of Seven with the smallest prime number greater than Five is therefore wrongly adduced as an instance of strict identity. The identity of Seven with the smallest prime number greater than Five relates to systematic existents, which are known a priori, and so it gives no insight into a kind of identity that allegedly obtains between empirical existents, which are known a posteriori. The statement of a numerical identity is analytic, whereas the statement of a strict identity is synthetic.

Consider the three instances of contingent identity. Smart denies that the identity between the successful general and the small boy who stole the apples is a strict identity, though he asserts that each is a time slice of the same four-dimensional object. Now, the reason why he denies that the identity is strict seems to be just that although both the general and the boy are time slices of that four-dimensional object, they are different time slices of it. That is, they are not slices of it at the same time. Thus, although a king may bestow the Order of the Black Rose on the successful general, he does not thereby bestow it also on the small boy who stole the apples. But suppose that the successful general

[3] *Ibid.*, p. 145.

is identical with the only bearded general in the kingdom. Then, when the king bestows the Order of the Black Rose on the successful general, he thereby bestows it on the only bearded general in the kingdom. What is the difference between these two identities? The successful general is only spatiotemporally continuous with the small boy, whereas he is spatiotemporally coincident with the only bearded general in the kingdom. This point about spatiotemporal coincidence being necessary for there to be strict identity is borne out by Smart's reluctance to say that the Morning Star and the Evening Star are strictly identical. The substantive expressions 'The Morning Star' and 'The Evening Star' are in fact used to designate the same thing, but continuous observation of what is designated by the one is required over a considerable duration for someone to ascertain that it is identical with what is designated by the other. This continuity of observation is like that necessary for someone to ascertain that the small boy who stole the apples is identical with the successful general. But no such continuity of observation is required for anyone to ascertain that the successful general and the only bearded general in the kingdom are identical. For given the descriptive expressions 'the successful general' and 'the only bearded general in the kingdom', someone who points to an object and tells us that the first expression designates it can immediately thereafter tell us that the second expression designates it also. In view of this I offer this definition of 'strict identity': If something, x, has certain spatiotemporal co-ordinates, then something, y, is strictly identical with x if, and only if, y has the same spatiotemporal co-ordinates as x.

Smart's fourth example of strict identity, namely the identity of a flash of lightning with an electrical discharge to the earth from a cloud of ionized water-molecules, confirms the foregoing analysis of 'strict identity'. For the flash and the discharge have the same spatiotemporal co-ordinates.

Because it is extremely important to have a clear understanding of strict identity I give one more example, even at the risk of taxing the reader's patience. Consider the sentence, 'The author of *Waverly* is identical with Walter Scott.' This sentence expresses an identity of the sort Smart had in mind, for there is one and only one person who is an author of *Waverly*, and this person is Walter Scott. But it is only contingent that Walter Scott is the author of *Waverly*. Indeed, in principle there might be a Walter Scott but no *Waverly*, or *Waverly* but no Walter Scott. Walter Scott's identity with the author of *Waverly* is known *a posteriori* and is a contingent identity. And it is an identity of just this sort that Smart asserts to obtain between an experience and a brain-state or brain-process.

Malcolm[4] believes that Smart's identity theory is not even false, but that it is unintelligible. Malcolm discusses the situation in which someone suddenly remembers that he has not put out his empty milk bottles to be collected. According to the identity theory, this sudden thought is strictly identical with some brain-state or brain-process of the person's. Such a state or process is a mechanical, chemical, or electrical state or process in his brain substance, or an electrical discharge from his brain mass, etc., and accordingly occurs inside his skull. Now, Malcolm states that "in our ordinary use of the terms 'thought' and 'thinking', we attach no meaning to the notion of determining the bodily location of a thought . . . we should have no idea what to look for to settle [the question where a thought is located bodily]" (118). He continues:

> In [sic] might be replied that *as things are* the bodily location of thoughts is not a meaningful notion; but if massive correlations [sic!] were discovered between thoughts and brain processes then we might *begin* to locate thoughts in the head. To this I must answer that our philosophical problem *is* about how things are. It is a question about our *present* concepts of thinking and thought not about some conjectured future concepts. (119)

Notice first that Malcolm clearly begs the principal question by writing of "correlations" between thoughts and brain-processes. For since it makes no sense to speak of correlating a thing with itself, only if thoughts and brain-processes are *not* identical can there be correlations between them. He should make his point about the so-called correlations by stating that if it is discovered

---

4 Norman Malcolm, "Scientific Materialism and the Identity Theory", *Dialogue*, III, 2 (1964), pp. 115-125.

that whatever a thought-expression denotes is also denoted by some brain-process-expression and *vice versa*, then we may begin to locate thoughts in the head.

Moreover, Malcolm confuses "how things are" with what "our present concepts" are, that is, with how things are presently said to be. Surely it is logically possible that our present concepts do not adequately analyze how things are and that these concepts ought therefore to be revised or renounced. By writing disparagingly about "conjectured future concepts", Malcolm makes it seem as though conjectured future concepts cannot adequately analyze how things are. But this is a mistake, for there is nothing sacrosanct about present concepts or sinister about future concepts in virtue of which the former necessarily be used to analyze how things are or even be preferred to the latter. Malcolm overlooks an important point that Hampshire states quite forcefully:

> In the ordinary use of language, and until philosophical doubts arise, every type of description in any language is accepted as having its own appropriate conditions of certainty and its own appropriate method of confirmation. . . . A philosopher in effect says: 'I know of course that these are the conditions which are ordinarily taken as the standard conditions for the use of expressions of this type: but can we ever be certain about the application of any expression of this type, in the sense in which we can have certainty in the application of expressions of this other type?' In asking this question, he is in effect challenging the accepted rules of application for the family of expressions considered; he is suggesting that the concept is otiose. . . .[5]

The family of expressions may drop out of the language and be replaced by others that have clearer and more definite conventions of application.

Malcolm is guilty of having an exaggerated respect for established usage. Philosophers begin their conceptual analyses by referring to ordinary-language usages. Indeed, where else can conceptual analyses begin? But a conceptual analysis may show some familiar concept to be unworthy of acceptance, because it is vague or even unintelligible. One example: Quite often, laymen speak of "the universe" and its properties. Even philosophers do.

---

[5] Stuart Hampshire, "The Interpretation of Language: Words and Concepts", in C. A. Mace, ed., *British Philosophy in the Mid-Century*, 1957, p. 275.

Indeed, Moore believes that the most important and interesting thing philosophers try to do is "to give a description of the *whole* of the Universe."[6] Consider, however, this passage from a lecture by Russell:[7]

> [This] view would make the universe itself the subject of various predicates which could not be applied to any particular thing in the universe, and the ascription of such peculiar predicates to the universe would be the special business of philosophy. I maintain, on the contrary, that there are no propositions of which the "universe" is the subject; in other words, that there is no such thing as the "universe." What I do maintain is that there are general propositions which may be asserted of each individual thing, such as the propositions of logic. This does not involve that all the things there are form a whole which could be regarded as another thing and be made the subject of predicates. It involves only the assertion that there are properties which belong to each separate thing, not that there are properties belonging to the whole of things collectively. (110-111)

My point here is not to decide whether Russell is right or Moore is right about the intelligibility of statements about "the whole universe". Rather, my point is merely to emphasize that the upshot of philosophical analysis sometimes is to advocate conceptual reform, which manifests itself in a change in linguistic usage. As Russell may be wrong vis-a-vis Moore, so Smart may be wrong vis-a-vis a non-materialist. But it is a mistake to believe, as Malcolm apparently does, that the mere fact that established linguistic usage attaches no meaning to 'the bodily location of a thought' is itself sufficient to warrant our asserting that Smart's identity theory is unintelligible.

There are other reasons why Malcolm asserts that Smart's identity theory is unintelligible. Malcolm points out that "a thought requires circumstances" (120) and he asserts that those required by the milk-bottle thought are "the existence of an organized community, of a practice of collecting and distributing milk bottles, of a rule that empty bottles will not be collected unless placed outside the door, and so on" (120). According to Smart, everything in the world is explicable in terms of physics

---

6 George Edward Moore, *Some Main Problems of Philosophy*, 1953, p. 1.

7 Bertrand Russell, "On Scientific Method in Philosophy", reprinted in *Mysticism and Logic*, 1917, pp. 97-124.

and so someone's sudden thought about the milk bottles is explicable in terms of physics. But Malcolm believes that to explain the occurrence of the thought one must then be able to describe in terms of physics the circumstances without which that thought is unintelligible. He writes:

> If the identity theory were true, then the surroundings [circumstances] that are [conceptually] necessary for the existence of my sudden thought would also be [empirically] necessary for the existence of the brain process with which it is identical. That brain process would not have occurred unless, for example, there was or had been a practice of delivering milk [and a rule that empty bottles will not be collected unless placed outside the door]. (121)

But these circumstances, according to Malcolm, cannot be described in terms of physics. Indeed, he doubts "that anyone knows what it would mean to say, for example, that the *rule* that milk bottles will not be collected unless placed outside the door is a configuration of ultimate particles" (122-123).

But it is not the rule, but a person's recognizing the rule that is alleged to be a configuration of ultimate particles. Malcolm himself writes of "the brain substance" and "the brain mass" and thereby takes the brain to be a four-dimensional space-time solid. This solid consists of connected neurons, which themselves consist of nucleic acids, proteins, water, and other chemicals, which in turn consist of atoms. The atoms are composed of protons, electrons, neutrons, and other elementary particles. Now, according to Smart's identity theory, the neural pathways of the brain are configurations of elementary particles. Consequently, we should inquire into what relationship can in principle obtain between these neural pathways and a person's recognizing a rule, not between the pathways and the rule itself.

Any stimulus that initiates a pattern of activity in the central nervous system produces a slight modification of the tissues over which the impulse passes. When a similar stimulus is presented, the already modified tissues facilitate the impulse's passing over the same pathway. And the more frequently the similar stimuli are presented and the shorter the interval between presentations, the greater is the degree of facilitation. Thus, repeated enunciation of a rule in perceptual circumstances appropriate to its application may produce an engram in the brain substance. This engram would be associated with stimili of a specific type and with utterances stating the rule. These utterances would be recognized to have a certain prescriptive force, which would consist in the tone in which they are uttered and in certain other memory associations, which likewise are cortical engrams. Some of the same neurons that compose the rule-engram would compose the tone- and other memory-engrams. Lashley expressly states that a cortical neuron belongs to more than one engram.[8] Fusion of these simple engrams would constitute a contextual background for any one of them. In Malcolm's example, an empty milk bottle would be a visual stimulus that initiates activity in the brain causing the brain-process that Smart would identify with Malcolm's "sudden thought", and the background for this thought would be the rest of the composite engram of which the thought's engram is part. And so, given that particular engrams are particular configurations of ultimate particles, a person's recognizing a rule would be a particular configuration of particles. Of course, I am not contending that neurophysiologists are presently able to pinpoint things this accurately. I am contending only that this account is at least intelligible and that Malcolm therefore is mistaken to object that saying that a person's recognizing a rule is a configuration of ultimate particles is unintelligible.

Malcolm also argues that 'to explain' is an intentional verb, so if x is merely strictly identical with y, strict identity being a contingent relationship, to explain x is not to explain y and to explain y is not to explain x. Hence, even if a thought is strictly identical with a brain-state or a brain-process, to explain the existence of the brain-state or the occurrence of the brain-process is not to explain the existence or occurrence of thought. The explanations, he emphasizes, belong to different systems of explanation.

But Malcolm misconstrues the intentionality of 'to explain'. Even if the identity theory is sound, it is linguistically odd to explain a thought in terms of configurations of ultimate particles, though it is not linguistically odd to explain a brain-state or a brain-process in terms of configurations of ultimate particles. But this is simply because the linguistic idiom in which 'a thought' is used is wholly separate from the linguistic idiom in which 'a

---

[8] K. S. Lashley, "In Search of the Engram", *Symposia of the Society of Experimental Biology*, 4: 454-482 (1950).

configuration of ultimate particles' is used. Parallel linguistic oddities derive, for instance, from a mixture of the sense-datum idiom and the ordinary physical-object idiom: 'A locomotive runs on sense-data' and 'The man struck a match and lighted one of the ends of the cylindrical sense-datum he held between his lips'. These sentences would be odd even if it were agreed that physical objects are strictly identical with compounds of sense-data, the latter being understood to be empirically ascertainable entities. Or consider this unproblematic identity: the temperature of a gas is strictly identical with the mean kinetic energy of the gas molecules. Now, although we say that *the temperature of the gas* is 75° centigrade it is linguistically odd to say that *the mean kinetic energy of the gas molecules* is 75° centigrade.

'A locomotive' and 'the temperature' are ordinary-language expressions, whereas 'sense-data' and 'mean kinetic energy' are theory-laden expressions. Expressions using 'sense-data' putatively analyze the ordinary-language descriptive expression 'a locomotive'; and expressions using 'mean kinetic energy' putatively explain whatever is denoted by the ordinary-language descriptive expression 'the temperature'. The putative analysis of the descriptive expression 'a locomotive' uses allegedly descriptive expressions of *a perceptual* theory which are said to be logically entailed by that expression and jointly to entail it logically. The putative explanation of what is denoted by the ordinary-language descriptive expression 'the temperature', namely the hotness recorded on a definite scale, uses allegedly descriptive expressions of *a physical theory* which are said to entail that descriptive expression nomologically. The analysis and the explanation obviously employ some ordinary-language expressions, such as 'the', 'of', 'is', etc., but neither employs only ordinary-language expressions. Indeed, except for using ordinary-language descriptive expressions to mention what is being analyzed and explained, the analysis and the explanation use theory-laden descriptive expressions only.

To return to Malcolm's example, the expression 'a thought' is an ordinary-language expression, whereas 'a configuration of ultimate particles' is a theory-laden expression. In advocating the identity theory, the materialist is analyzing the ordinary-language descriptive expression 'a thought' in terms of theoretical expressions of physics. His analysis is part of an epistemological theory. The phenomenological report 'I had a sudden thought' should be construed neutrally between a non-spatial account of a thought and the materialist account that assigns a bodily location to it. A *description* of the thought mentions, for instance, that it was sudden, suddenness being a relational property of the thought. An *explanation* of the thought's having occurred mentions something, x, other than the thought, and the relationship between the thought and x, for instance, the visual stimulus of an empty milk bottle. And an *analysis* of the thought also mentions something other than the thought, for instance, the configurations of ultimate particles. The description, the explanation, and the analysis are three distinguishable things and are instances of three different kinds of linguistic activity. Malcolm overlooks this point and in so doing fails to see that the oddity of saying that to explain a brain-process is to explain the thought with which it allegedly is strictly identical derives from mixing expressions that do not belong together because they are appropriate to different ranges of discourse. The materialist does not contend that 'a thought' and 'a brain-process' have the same logic, but only that as a matter of fact they have the same extension. Accordingly, there is no reason to expect that these expressions be mutually substitutable even when they are not preceded by an intentional verb. Thus, although we can say that a configuration of ultimate particles is geometrically elliptical, it is linguistically odd to say that a thought is geometrically elliptical; and ' . . . is geometrically elliptical' is an extensional context.

Moreover, Malcolm is mistaken about whether or not to explain the occurrence of a brain-process is to explain the occurrence of a thought, assuming that the thought *is* strictly identical with the brain-process. For suppose that I know which configuration of ultimate particles the brain-process is and also which is strictly identical with that brain-process. Then I know which configuration of ultimate particles is strictly identical with that thought. And if my physical theory is sufficiently advanced to permit me to explain and to predict the occurrence of that configuration of ultimate particles, then since I know which thought is strictly identical with that configuration, my physical theory permits me to explain and to predict the occurrence of the thought. I can explain and predict its occurrence solely on the basis of my physical theory of brain-processes, the identity theory, and a description of relevant states of affairs obtaining at some finite time prior to its occurrence. To be sure, a sentence such as 'My thought that I should put the empty milk bottles outside my door to be collected was caused by a 200 millivolt impulse to the cortical center X' is linguistically odd, whereas the sentence 'The configuration of ultimate particles, C, in my brain was caused by a 200 millivolt impulse to cortical center X' is not. But that is no reason to say that even if I know that the thought and the configuration are strictly identical I do not know what caused the thought. For if my theory permits me nomologically to derive the statement describing my thought from statements describing my brain-processes, then by mentioning the occurrence of whatever my brain-process-statements describe I do explain the occurrence of whatever my thought-statement describes. The fact that my nomological sentence does not itself use the expression 'my thought' or describe my thought, but uses the expression 'the configuration of ultimate particles, C' or describes the configuration is not to the point. For the explanation of the thought's occurrence is not merely the nomological sentence but that sentence together with the sentence strictly identifying the configuration and the thought. In short, the explanation is the nomological sentence and the identity sentence. Malcolm errs by taking only the nomological sentence to be the explanation and by therefore inferring that no genuine explanation of the thought's occurrence is given since neither 'the thought' nor a description of the thought occurs in that sentence. Whether or not the occurrence of a thought can be explained by a physical theory cannot be decided on the basis of the linguistic point that neither names nor descriptions of thoughts appear in the sentences of that theory.

Malcolm adduces one more argument against the theory that a thought and a brain-process are strictly identical. He writes:

> Suppose we had determined, by means of some instrument, that a certain process occurred inside my skull at the exact moment I had the sudden thought about the milk bottles. How do we make the further test of whether my *thought* occurred inside my skull? For it would have to be a *further* test: it would have to be logically independent

of the test for the presence of the brain process, because Smart's
thesis is that the identity is *contingent*. But no one has any notion of
what it would mean to test for the occurrence of the thought inside
my skull *independently* of testing for a brain process. The idea of such
a test is not intelligible. (119-120)

Malcolm's point here is that if the same evidence that establishes that a certain process occurred inside his skull establishes
that the thought that allegedly is strictly identical with the process occurred inside his skull, and *vice versa,* the evidence that
one occurred inside his skull is not logically independent of the
evidence that the other occurred inside his skull. This being so,
the test for one occurrence's being inside his skull is not logically
independent of the test for the other occurrence's being inside
his skull. But since the identity between the occurrences is contingent the tests must be logically independent of each other.
And since they are not, the putative identity is unintelligible.

It is difficult to understand why Malcolm wants to test for a
thought's being inside his skull, for in one of the articles by
Smart to which Malcolm refers, Smart writes that he is not identifying a brain-process with an after-image, but with the *experience* of having an after-image; and it is reasonable to believe
that Smart does not identify a brain-process with a thought, but
with the experience of thinking that thought.[9] And if what is
reasonable to believe also is true, then the experience and not
the thought should concern Malcolm. Of course, Malcolm can
and should make the same point about locating the experience
inside his skull as he makes about locating the thought inside
his skull.

I do not see how Smart can reply adequately to this objection.
He cannot admit psychic entities into his system, for at best
they would be nomological danglers. And he cannot reduce so-
called psychic properties to physical properties, for to do that
would be to define the former in terms of the latter, which
would change strict identity from a contingent to a conceptual
relationship. Shaffer[10] seems to overlook these points when he

---

[9] J. J. C. Smart, "Sensations and Brain Processes", p. 150.
[10] Jerome Shaffer, "Could Mental States Be Brain Processes?", *The Journal
of Philosophy,* LVIII, 26 (1961), reprinted in G. N. A. Vesey, ed., *Body and
Mind,* 1964, pp. 450-459.

writes that he sees "no reason why the Identity theorist should be disconcerted by admitting that psychic properties are different from physical properties" (456). Nor can Smart argue as follows.[11] The statement assigning a location to a thought embodies a category-mistake, so there is no point in testing for a thought's occurring inside someone's skull. A brain-process x, and a thought, y, may significantly be said not to be identical if, and only if, for some property F, 'Fx' is true but 'Fy' is false, or *vice versa*. For this situation to obtain even in principle, 'F' must in principle be predictable of 'y'. But this condition cannot be satisfied if 'Fy' is a category-mistake. Hence, the question of identity or non-identity does not arise, for to say that a thought occurs inside someone's skull is to commit a category-mistake. Smart cannot reply this way, because the argument ignores the definition of 'strict identity' and the requirement of strict identity between experience and brain-process.

At the outset of this chapter I remarked that one of the objections to the theory that someone's mental events or experiences are identical with certain events or processes in his brain warrants rejecting the theory. The objection I had in mind is Malcolm's objection about testing to establish that someone's experience, in contradistinction to the brain-process that allegedly is strictly identical with it, occurs inside that person's skull. But rejecting Smart's theory does not entail asserting a non-materialistic conception of mind, for there is a materialistic conception of mind other than Smart's. I shall therefore defend a theory that differs from his.

According to this second materialistic conception of mind, some one's having an experience is identical with his being in a certain brain-state or undergoing a certain brain-process. The identity obtains between two states of affairs, to wit, the person's *having* a certain experience and his *being in* a certain brain-state or his *undergoing* a certain-process. For the identity to obtain he must have the experience when he is in the brain-state or undergoes the brain-process. The state of affairs denoted by an experience-expression and that denoted by its corresponding neurophysiological-expression must obtain at the same time if

---

11 Cf. James W. Cornman, "The Identity of Mind and Body", *The Journal of Philosophy*, LIX, 18 (1962), pp. 486-492.

the expressions are to denote the same thing. And the state of affairs denoted by one expression must obtain at the same place as that denoted by the other expression if the expressions are to denote the same thing. In short, the relevant kind of identity is strict identity.

It may be objected to begin with that it makes no sense to say that states of affairs are strictly identical, because they do not have spatial coordinates. A thing may be said to have a location, but a state of affairs, it will be objected, may not be said to have a location. I think that this objection is mistaken. Admittedly, a state of affairs differs from a thing. But consider the state of affairs consisting in the temperature's being 65° Fahrenheit in the room in which I am writing this sentence at time T. Where does this state of affairs obtain? Surely there is an answer to this question, to wit: wherever the room is in which I am writing the relevant sentence at time T. To speak of the spatial coordinates of that room is perfectly meaningful, and so to speak of the state of affairs that obtains in that room is perfectly meaningful. Similarly, my writing the relevant sentence at time T is a state of affairs. And it too can meaningfully be assigned the location specified by the spatial co-ordinates of the room. Thus, it makes sense to say that states of affairs are strictly identical, for they may be assigned the same spatiotemporal co-ordinates.

It is advisable to begin by considering this theory in the light of the criticism that led to abandoning its predecessor. For Smart's theory to be intelligible, someone's experience of thinking a thought must occur inside that person's skull (where the allegedly strictly identical brain-process occurs), and the test for the experience's occurring inside his skull must differ from the test for the brain-process' occurring inside his skull. Malcolm argues that no independent test can be devised to establish that the experience occurs inside the skull, so Smart's theory is unsound. Does my theory fare better against this criticism? I believe that it does. First, there is an important difference between 'being in a certain brain-state' or 'undergoing a certain brain-process' and 'brain-state' or 'brain-process', to wit, that whereas the latter two expressions denote what is locatable inside someone's skull, the former two expressions denote what is locatable

no more precisely than wherever some person is. The expressions
'P's having a certain experience' and 'P's being in a certain brain-
state or undergoing a certain brain-process' have the same extension; and what they denote is locatable just where P is. No
more precise location for these strictly identical states of affairs
can be specified than that of being where P is. Accordingly, and
second, there can be a test for a certain experience's occurring
where P is that is independent of the test for a certain brain-
state's or brain-process' occurring where P is. Thus, we may
follow Malcolm in supposing that we can ascertain, by means
of some instrument, that a person's brain is in a certain state
or is undergoing a certain process. We may then call these a
brain-state and a brain-process, respectively; and we may say
that the person is in the brain-state or is undergoing the brain-
process. Here, the test is neurophysiological. Now, in ordinary
circumstances, a person's reporting that he is having a certain
experience suffices for us to state that he is having it. By 'ordinary circumstances' is meant his being a fluent or at least a
native speaker of the language in which he utters the report,
his being honest, there being no advantage in his lying, there
occurring no slip of his tongue, etc. Clearly, his reporting that
he is having a certain experience differs from the neurophysiological evidence that he is in a certain brain-state or is undergoing
a certain brain-process. Hence, the tests to establish that someone is in a certain brain-state or undergoing a certain brain-
process and that he is having a certain experience are mutually
independent, as Malcolm rightly requires them to be.

An essential feature of my theory is that the report of having
an experience be what Smart calls "topic-neutral", that is, that
the report have the following form: 'There is now occurring in
me, or there just occurred in me, a process, x, such that x is like
what occurs in me when such-and-such a physical stimulus affects
me.' This form requires that neither a mental event nor a brain
event be mentioned and that only physicalistic terms of ordinary-language discourse be used. Then, whatever satisfies the
description 'x is like . . .' is empirically ascertainable, for the
description states conditions under which a determinate mental
phenomenon contingently occurs. Thus, if I report that my right
hand hurts, then topic-neutrally I say, "There is now occurring

in me a process like that which occurs in me when my hand is struck with a hard object." This expression is not a translation of the statement 'My right hand hurts', for obviously I might have learned the concept of my right hand's hurting me without it having been struck with a hard object. Nevertheless, sensation-terminology is learned by reference to some environmental stimulus, even if not necessarily to any particular one.

Suppose someone objects that this is all right for sensation-terminology but not for thought-terminology. It does seem that the experience of feeling a pain can be described topic-neutrally because sensation-terminology, of which pain-terminology is a sub-division, is learned by reference to environmental stimuli, whereas the experience of thinking a thought cannot be so described, because thought-terminology is not learned by reference to environmental stimuli. But this objection is answerable. A thought, as was remarked above, requires surroundings. And similarly, thinking requires surroundings. We ordinarily have no difficulty in recognizing someone's utterance as pertinent to an inquiry or in recognizing his action as intellectual. Thus, if an inspector investigating a murder asks whether or not fingerprints have been found on the murder weapon, or if someone laughs at a ridiculous incident, we recognize his behavior as "mental". To say that the inspector is now wondering whether or not fingerprints have been found on the murder weapon, or that someone is now amused at the ridiculous incident although he is not laughing is to say, topic-neutrally, that what is occurring in the inspector is like what occurs in him when, while investigating a murder, he asks whether or not fingerprints have been found on the murder weapon, or that what is occurring in the other person is like what occurs in him when he laughs at the ridiculous incident. Lest it be objected that these formulations sound as though the inspector habitually asks whether or not fingerprints have been found on that weapon and the other person habitually laughs at that ridiculous incident, let it be understood that 'asks' and 'laughs' occur in the formulations as occasion-terms, not habit-terms.

It may be contended that the foregoing analysis is inadequate because we cannot talk of "surroundings" in an exclusively materialistic context. Thus, someone may declare that it would be

a mistake to regard human beings as merely very complex physico-chemical mechanisms and their behavior as explicable in terms
of causal necessitation, because understanding their behavior requires such distinctive notions as 'purpose' and 'rationality', etc.,
none of which can be explicated physico-chemically. This appears
to be the point of the following argument by Ryle.[12]

> Physicists may one day have found the answers to all physical ques-
> tions, but not all questions are physical questions. . . . The favorite
> model to which the fancied mechanistic world is assimilated is that of
> billiard balls imparting their motion to one another by impact. Yet
> a game of billiards provides one of the simplest examples of a course
> of events for the description of which mechanical terms are necessary
> without being sufficient. Certainly from accurate knowledge of the
> weight, shape, elasticity and movements of the balls, the constitution
> of the table and the conditions of the atmosphere it is in principle
> possible, in accordance with known laws, to deduce from a momentary
> state of the balls what will be their later state. But it does not follow
> from this that the course of the game is predictable in accordance
> with those laws alone. A scientific forecaster, who was ignorant of the
> rules and tactics of the game and of the skill and plans of the players,
> could predict, perhaps, from the beginning of a single stroke, the
> positions in which the balls will come to rest before the next stroke is
> made; but he could predict no further. . . . Mechanism then is a mere
> bogy. . . .

First, Ryle begs the question by tacitly assuming that we
cannot have accurate knowledge of the player's brain-states or
brain-processes, or that if we can, such knowledge, together
with accurate knowledge of the environmental influences on the
player and the knowledge Ryle himself mentions, is insufficient
to predict the stroke itself. At any rate, he does not mention this
additional knowledge, so his argument is not to the mechanist's
point. Second, I admit that 'purpose' and 'rationality' cannot be
analyzed merely physico-chemically. But whether or not they can
be is irrelevant to whether or not a purely physico-chemical
mechanism can behave purposively and rationally. The fact that
non-physical terms such as 'purpose' and 'rationality' are not
translatable into physical terms is irrelevant to my identity
theory, just as it is to Smart's, for my thesis too is about facts,

---

12 Gilbert Ryle, *The Concept of Mind*, 1949, pp. 76, 79-80, and 81.

not meanings. The issue is not whether or not the terms are translatable, but whether or not a purely physico-chemical mechanism can behave purposively and rationally. Third, and closely related to the second point, although certain ongoings of a human organism, for instance playing chess or drawing a bank check, cannot be explained solely in physical terms, it does not follow that these ongoings do not have physically sufficient conditions. Nor is it true that "absolutely nothing about any matter of human conduct follows logically from any account of the physiological conditions of bodily movement."[13] Thus, although one cannot explain a chess move without understanding the concepts of a game, or rules, etc. or explain someone's drawing a bank check without understanding certain legal, economic, and social conventions, by referring to the physical conditions sufficient for the occurrence of the bodily movements involved in performing the relevant action, one can explain the occurrence of these movements. And if one describes only the physical movement involved in making a certain chess move or the physiologically sufficient conditions of these physical movements, the description does logically entail that the player whose movements they are is not making a certain chess move. A description that includes only a physiological account of his bodily movements and a physical account of moving only the smallest piece of wood on the board entails his neither castling nor chess-moving the king. Yet the description is a purely physical description of a situation and the statement about his chess move not being either of the two mentioned is something more than a mere physical description. Similarly a complete or nearly complete physiological account of someone's high-jumping logically entails that he is not bowing when the account accurately describes the sufficient conditions of his contemporaneously occurring bodily movements. It is true, however, that a description such as the one just mentioned cannot entail that a certain action is being performed, for instance that a certain chess move is being made. But this is only because different conceptual schemes are used, one to describe bodily movements and the other to describe actions. And this difference in *conceptual* schemes is irrelevant to a strict identity thesis, which is a contention about a *factual* matter.

---

[13] A. I. Melden, *Free Action*, 1961, p. 201.

Quite besides the foregoing objection about explaining all human action physico-chemically, someone may object that the concepts of rationality and validity are unintelligible, given my identity theory. He may argue, more specifically, that the concept of a good reason or a valid argument disappears if we accept a causal explanation of belief, for if beliefs are caused there is no sense in speaking of reasonable beliefs or valid arguments. This objection, however, confuses the neurophysiological conditions under which we accept a belief with the meaning of 'belief'. But whether we analyze 'a belief' as an abstract entity of some sort or as a disposition to perform certain specifiable acts under certain specifiable conditions, there may be neurophysiological conditions sufficient for a belief to exist or to obtain. Whether or not a belief is reasonable or an argument valid depends on conditions different in kind from these neurophysiological conditions. If someone states, for instance, that since X is the son of Y, Y must be X's father, we can point out that his argument is fallacious, for Y may be X's mother. Y's being X's mother is a possibility that is independent of the neurophysiological conditions sufficient for the person to state his argument, as is the rule that for his argument to be valid the allegedly entailed proposition must be the only possible proposition specifying X's immediate ancestry. Thus, the conditions for the validity or reasonableness of an argument are independent of the neurophysiological conditions sufficient for someone's stating the argument. Smart observes that if we sometimes discount a person's remark because we can assign some cause for it, such as a lesion of the brain, it is surely because we have noticed that this condition frequently is associated with irrationality.[14] Similarly, a neurophysiologist may be able to establish that someone's testimony is not reasonable by explaining that the person's occipital or visual cortex is damaged enough to impair his visual memory. Asked, for instance, whether or not the driver in a certain accident could have avoided the pedestrian he struck, the person's answer, though perhaps correct, cannot be well-grounded since he cannot visualize the accident. He has lost the capacity to make certain kinds of judgment, viz. reports of what did happen and estimates of what might have happened, insofar as they are

---

[14] J. J. C. Smart, *Philosophy and Scientific Realism*, p. 127

based on visual recollection. In this instance, unlike the one about a lesion of the brain, we do not have a correlation between a type of brain condition and unreasonable argument; rather, we know that the person no longer has a certain capacity and that since exercising this capacity is necessary for judgments of certain kinds to be reasonable his judgments of these kinds are not reasonable. In both instances we have neurophysiological evidence relevant to the reasonableness of belief, although the criterion of reasonableness itself is not neurophysiological.

Another objection that may be raised against my theory is this. The identity theory states that a mechanistic account of experience is possible in that if we discover a type of brain-state or brain-process and establish that it is invariably concomitant with a certain type of experience, we can formulate an identity law: 'Whenever someone is in a brain-state of type BS^1, or is undergoing a brain-process of type BP^1, then he is having an experience of type E^1; and whenever someone is having an experience of type E^1, then he is in a brain-state of type BS^1 or is undergoing a brain-process of type BP^1.' In short, the identity theory states that a person's having a specific experience of a certain type is inferable from his being in a specific brain-state of a certain type or his undergoing a specific brain-process of a certain type. But according to the objector, this theory is unsound because the inference requires using a statement in which a mentalistic expression occurs, namely, the expression 'experience of type E^1'.

In fact, however, the objection itself is unsound, for the expression 'experience of type E^1' is not mentalistic, but neutral. The report 'I am now having an experience of type E^1' or 'I just had an experience of type E^1' leaves open what kind of ongoing is being reported. Even if the report were properly understood to be of a mentalistic event, its being so understood would be a matter of its being made in the ordinary-language idiom. The materialistic theory changes the meaning of the so-called mentalistic expression and makes it topic-neutral. The theory correlates the speech-act or report with a concomitant brain-state or brain-process of a certain type. That in so doing it changes the meaning of the so-called mentalistic expression is not a defect in the identity theory any more than Einstein's modifications of

Newtonian concepts are a defect in relativity theory. The important thing to notice is that the correlation is between someone's *speech-act* of reporting his having a certain experience and his being in a brain-state of a certain type or his undergoing a brain-process of a certain type. The correlation is not between the *meaning* of 'an experience of type E¹' and something. Indeed, I cannot see any point in trying to correlate meanings with states of a living organism.

Using the expression 'a living organism' is important in distinguishing my theory from Smart's. He envisions the possibility that a human brain is kept alive *in vitro* and he contends that the occurrence of certain processes in the brain warrants our saying that the brain thinks. On my theory, someone's thinking is identical with his being in a certain brain-state or undergoing a certain brain-process, not with the brain-state or brain-process itself, so I attach no meaning to the expression 'the brain is thinking'. On Smart's theory, a *brain* is described as being in a certain state or undergoing a certain process, whereas on my theory, a *person* is described as being in a certain brain-state or undergoing a certain brain-process. My theory therefore requires less revision of ordinary-language than Smart's does and so is more convenient than his. Of course, the degree of required revision is merely a matter of convenience and not of soundness.

I shall now summarize my brain-mind identity theory and briefly state why it is preferable to its alternatives. I contend that someone's having an experience is strictly identical with his being in a certain brain-state or his undergoing a certain brain-process. The expression 'having a certain experience' is not synonymous with the expression 'being in a certain brain-state' or 'undergoing a certain brain-process' but has the same extension as they have. The only thing that has an experience is a living organism and the only thing that is in a brain-state or that undergoes a brain-process is a living organism. The state of affairs of having a certain experience, of being in a certain brain-state, or of undergoing a certain brain-process is wherever the organism is. The location assigned to the state of affairs cannot be made any more precise than that. I advocate this theory because it is simpler than any of its alternatives. Its simplicity consists essentially in its needing fewer sorts of thing to account for the facts of experience, for instance its not needing irreducibly "psychic" entities or properties in addition to bodily states and processes and so not needing any laws linking such entities or properties with bodily states and processes. Surely, as Smart points out, if a materialistic theory of mind is intelligible, then it is incumbent on anyone who disputes it to produce a concept of an entity or property that is an irreducibly "psychic" entity or property.[15] And I have presented an intelligible materialistic theory of mind.

[15] J. J. C. Smart, *Philosophy and Scientific Realism*, p. 105.

CHAPTER V

Knowledge of Other Minds

O would I were where I would be!
There would I be where I am not:
For where I am I would not be,
And where I would be I can not.
—*Nursery Rhyme*

Everything is what it is, and not another thing.
—JOSEPH BUTLER, *Sermons*

If, as I have been contending, a person's having an experience is strictly identical with his being in a certain brain-state or his undergoing a certain brain-process, then the question whether or not an experience necessarily is someone's experience need not arise. Of course, if 'an experience' denotes something as 'a ticket' denotes something, then having an experience is like having a ticket to a concert insofar as there is a substant of a certain kind and someone who has the substant. But I do not use 'an experience' to denote a substant. Rather, I use it syncategorematically. The predicate expression 'is having an experience' does not attribute a relational attribute to a person; it attributes a qualitative attribute to him. Applying the predicate to some person indicates that he is qualitatively different from what he would be if he were not having an experience; applying it does not indicate that he stands in a relationship to something called 'an experience', in which relationship he does not stand unless that experience exists and he has it. Only a living organism can have an experi-

114

ence. I concern myself only with a sub-class of living organisms, to wit, living human beings. I shall discuss the so-called 'problem of other minds', which is a cluster of related issues, such as whether or not I can know that a putative person other than me has experiences, and if so, whether or not I can know what sort of experiences they are, etc.

Since speaking of experiences as being "owned" by a person is metaphorical, I want to state what I mean by ownership. There is an obvious sense in which we ordinarily construe the statement that a certain body is someone's. Imagine, for instance, several very young children playing the game of hiding under blankets and having one child run a hand over another's blanket and thereby try to ascertain who is under the blanket. Suppose that the child who is doing the touching accidentally touches the body of a child under a blanket, this being a violation of the rules. A referee might say: "You mustn't do that! Touch only his blanket, not his body!" Or consider the cinema dialogue: "If you want to know that, ask Sam."—"Sam's not talking anymore; the cops fished his body out of the river this morning." There is a relationship between Sam, for instance, and a certain body in virtue of which relationship we identify that body as his. This relationship is that of ownership. Now, a certain person's having a certain experience is strictly identical with a certain condition of a living human body, specifically the condition of its being in a certain brain-state or undergoing a certain brain-process. And since this body is owned by someone, so too are the experiences that are strictly identical with certain of the body's conditions. Thus, Sam's having been in a certain brain-state or undergone a certain brain-process is strictly identical with his having been afraid. The experience of being afraid, then, was owned by Sam when he had that brain-state or underwent that brain-process. It is in the foregoing sense only that I shall speak of an experience's being owned or its being someone's.

Can I know that a putative other-person is a person, that he is something more than an entity that merely looks and behaves like me in certain respects? Let us assume, for the argument's sake, that I do not accept the materialistic conception of mind advocated in the last chapter. There are philosophers who hold that I cannot then know whether or not a putative other-person has any experience whatever, or that if I assume he has experiences I cannot know what they are. Thomson[1] contends that there are two scepticisms about other minds, Weak Scepticism and Strong Scepticism.

> Weak Scepticism . . . is the view that we can never know what is in the mind of another, but that we may have good reason for thinking that he is feeling this or that . . . (21)
>
> Strong Scepticism . . . is the view that we can never know what is in the mind of another, and more, that we are never in a position even to have good reason for thinking he is feeling this or that—that any claim we make about what Smith is feeling can at best be a mere guess. (21)

The definition of 'Strong Scepticism' is thoroughly confused. To say "we *are never* in a position even to have a good reason . . ." entails that we *can be* in such a position. Hence, in the definition as stated, the contention "that any claim we make about what Smith is feeling can at best be a mere guess" means that the claim can at best be that because *as a matter of fact* we are never in a position to have a good reason. In other words, the expression following the dash in Thomson's definition of 'Strong Scepticism' is simply another way of saying we are never in a position to have a good reason. In amplifying her definition, however, Thomson states that it means we can never know what someone means by a sensation- or feeling-word "and that it is not conceivable that we should have any good reason for thinking he means [this or that]—any view we have as to what [the word] means can at best be a mere guess" (22). The clause just quoted is, of course, incompatible with her definition, for her definition states that it is merely a contingent matter that we never have a good reason to believe we know what the word means. There seem, then, to be more than two scepticisms:

> (A) We can never know what is in the mind of another but may have good reason to believe he is feeling this or that, and sometimes do have good reason to believe it.

---

[1] Judith Jarvis Thomson, "Private Languages", *American Philosophical Quarterly*, I: 20-31 (1964).

(B) We can never know what is in the mind of another, and although we may have good reason to believe he is feeling this or that, we never actually have it.

(C) We can never know what is in the mind of another and cannot even in principle have good reason to believe he is feeling this or that.

Now, (C), which is what I take Thomson to have intended by 'Strong Scepticism,' is self-contradictory, for saying we can *never* know something (a temporal term for a contingent state of affairs!) entails that we can in principle know it and so are not limited to mere guessing. Consequently, (C) should be replaced by

(D) We cannot even in principle know what is in the mind of another, but can only guess that he is feeling this or that, a guess being utterly arbitrary, i.e., not based on any evidence whatever.

Thomson regards the in principle impossibility of knowing what is in the mind of another person as different from, and as not entailing, our being limited in principle to mere guessing whether he is feeling this or that. She writes that

> with Strong Scepticism goes the view that we can never [sic] know what [another person] means by [a word] and that it is not conceivable that we should have any good reason for thinking he means "toothache" or anything else—any view we have as to what [the word] means can at best be a mere guess. (22)

Notice that she writes that Strong Scepticism comprises the beliefs that we can never (sic!) know what is in the mind of another person *and* that it is inconceivable that we should have any good reason for beilieving we know what he means by his sensation- or feeling-word. This is puzzling. For our necessarily being limited to mere guessing is identical with the logical impossibility of there being evidence for our belief that he is feeling this or that. Consequently, if the impossibility of knowing does not entail our being limited to mere guessing, it does not entail the impossibility of there being evidence for believing. Moreover, if the impossibility of knowing does not entail the impossibility of there being evidence for believing, then the impossibility of knowing is compatible with there being evidence for believing. And if the two are compatible, the expression 'it is logically impossible to know what is in the mind of another person' is very curious indeed. For if there can be evidence for believing that another person feels this or that, then *if* we can get *all* the evidence, we can *know* that he feels it. If we have all the evidence there is, then there is nothing for the lack of which we should be said not to know. But is it logically possible to get *all* the evidence? Perhaps what Thomson has in mind is that it is not. For there is one piece of evidence we cannot have, even in principle, namely the experience of the other person. Hence, although there may be evidence that he is feeling this or that, for instance his behavior is such evidence, we cannot even in principle *know* he is feeling this or that, because we cannot even in principle have his experience. But then, how does this contention differ from (A) and (B)? Well, neither (A) nor (B) states that it is logically impossible to know what is in the mind of another person, but only that we can never know it. If the 'can never' is supposed to mean 'it is logically impossible that,' as it does in Thomson's definition of 'Strong Scepticism,' then we should replace (A) and (B) by (E) and (F) respectively:

> (E) We cannot even in principle know what is in the mind of another person but can have good reason to believe he is feeling this or that and sometimes do have good reason to believe it.

> (F) We cannot even in principle know what is in the mind of another, and although we can in principle have good reason to believe he is feeling this or that we never actually have good reason to believe it.

Now, does (D) differ from (E) and (F)? On the contrary, (D) is identical with (E) or (F), depending on whether or not we ever have good reason to believe that another person is feeling this or that. There are, then, only two scepticisms, but not the two Thomson states. Rather, there are these two:

> (1) Weak Scepticism: We cannot even in principle know what is in the mind of another person; but we can in principle have good reason to believe he is feeling this or that, and we sometimes do have good reason to believe it.

> (2) Strong Scepticism: We cannot even in principle know what is in the mind of another person; and although we can in principle have good reason to believe he is feeling this or that, we never in fact have good reason to believe it.

The truth of (1) entails the falsity of (2), for if we sometimes have good reason to believe that another person is feeling this or that, then it is false that we never have good reason to believe it. Similiarly, the truth of (2) entails the falsity of (1), for if we never have good reason to believe that another person is feeling this or that, then we do not sometimes have good reason to believe it. But no valid inference about either (1) or (2) can be drawn from the falsity of either. For each is a compound statement, the first element of which is 'We cannot even in principle know what is in the mind of another'; and if the falsity of that element is what makes one statement false, it also makes the other statement false. On the other hand, if only the falsity of the second element makes one statement false, then the other statement is true, for the second elements are each other's formal contradictories.

In discussing Thomson's confusions I have followed her lead and spoken of whether or not "we" can know what is in the mind of "another person". In what follows I shall speak more strictly of whether or not *I* can know that *a putative other-person* is a person, and if so, what *I* can know about his experiences.

Why is there any issue whether or not I can know that a putative other-person is a person, that is, that an entity that looks and sounds and moves much as I do is the same sort of thing I am? Consider the sort of situation out of which the issue is conceived to arise. Suppose I show someone how to thrust with a foil and that, unknown to either of us, the button is missing from the point of the foil I use to demonstrate. Suppose further that when I thrust at him, the unbottoned foil pierces his skin, making him cry out. I immediately drop my foil and assist him, not doubting for a moment that he is in pain;—such is the exigency of the situation. But later, when his wound has been tended to and I have left him, I wonder whether or not my belief that he was in pain was warranted. I wonder whether or not I can know the thoughts, feelings, or sensations of another person, and if so, whether or not I ever do. I wonder whether or not I can know that an entity before me is a person, and if I can, whether or not I ever do. My knowing that something is a person is parasitical on my knowing that the something is shaped like a human being and exhibits human behavior, such as being in pain, thinking, etc. So let us look at the issue whether or not I can know that the human-like object whose skin my foil pierced was in pain.

Recall the circumstances in which I took him to be in pain. He had just been pierced by my foil and had cried out. There seem to be obvious reasons to say that when I am confronted by these circumstances I know him to be in pain: (1) there is a cause for a painful reaction, that is, there is a noxious stimulation, namely, my foil's piercing his flesh; (2) there is an inflammatory reaction at the site of stimulation (axon reflex); (3) there is a muscle reaction, namely, automatic withdrawal; (4) there is a glandular reaction, namely, perspiring; and finally, (5) there is the more highly integrated but still automatic adaptive pattern of quasi-purposive movement exhibited by respiratory reactions.

But then I hesitate, for clearly there is no necessary connection between 'Guildenstern is in pain' and any or all the statements of the kind I have given to support my belief that Guildenstern is in pain. The statement 'Guildenstern is in pain' does not entail any disjunction, nor is it entailed by any conjunction, of statements of the sort (a) 'Guildenstern says "Ouch",' or (b) "Guildenstern says that he is in pain', or (c) 'Guildenstern is bleeding'. For I certainly can imagine a situation in which he feels pain but does not manifest it to me in any way that would make any of the statements (1-5) or (a-c), which are true in the present situation, true in the imagined situation. And conversely, I can imagine a situation in which he manifests all these symptoms of being in pain but is not in fact feeling pain.

We sometimes speak of someone's being in pain but trying to conceal it. It may be that we say "he is *trying* to conceal it" rather than "he is concealing it" because if he succeeds in concealing it we should not know that he experiences it. But this does not mean that I cannot, without logical contradiction, imagine Guildenstern to be in pain but not to exhibit it in his behavior. Indeed, if we consider the converse example of an actor who is not in pain but who is required to play the role of someone who is in pain, we do not find it difficult to believe that he is able to do so. Why, then, since the same logic is involved, ought I to find any difficulty in believing that an actor or Guildenstern, who is in pain, can artfully conceal it and play the part of someone who is not in pain?

It is sometimes contended by people in my position that if Guildenstern says "I am in pain", he refers to a feeling of which he alone is conscious, his being conscious of it allegedly making it his. To be sure, he may also refer to certain publicly observable manifestations of pain, but if he does, they are not all his statement means. On the other hand, when I say of Guildenstern "He is in pain", all that my statement can mean is that he exhibits certain signs of pain or is disposed to behave in certain specific ways. Thus, what is alleged according to this contention is that the statement 'Guildenstern is in pain' has two meanings, depending upon whether it is asserted by Guildenstern or by someone else.

Now, if Guildenstern is asked how he knows he is in pain when he says "I am in pain", he can offer as a reason for his statement his experiencing a pain-sensation, his feeling a pain. He may also recognize certain outward circumstances (1-5), the pain-circumstances of his experience, but he distinguishes his feeling the pain from these circumstances; and his feeling the pain, not his recognizing the circumstances, is his evidence for the truth of his statement 'I am in pain'. But to support my statement that he is in pain, I can refer only to the pain-circumstances and especially to my observations of Guildenstern's outward behavior. I cannot refer to his feeling the pain, for I am not aware of the pain-sensation itself. Yet Guildenstern is aware of it even though I am not, which is to say that he can distinguish between his pain-sensation and the physical concomitants with which it is associated. But if it were correct to assert that the meaning of my statement 'Guildenstern is in pain' is only that he exhibits or is disposed to exhibit certain specific behavior patterns under certain specific conditions, then in distinguishing between his feeling and the expression of his feeling, he would commit the error of believing that the two kinds of expression refer to two different kinds of thing when in fact they refer to but one.

However, if I were to pierce my hand with a foil and were to say that I am in pain, I should be in the position with respect to myself that Guildenstern is in with respect to himself. It would then be meaningful for me to distinguish between my own pain-sensation or my own feeling of pain and its behavioral concomitants. But if I can make this distinction and I know I can make it in appropriate circumstances, I must acknowledge that it is a meaningful distinction even when Guildenstern makes it. For what is necessary for it to be meaningful is not that I should be in a position to make it, but that someone—anyone at all—be in such a position. The distinction between a pain-sensation or a feeling of pain and its outward concomitants is a meaningful distinction for any person, provided some person can be in a position to offer as a reason for the statement 'P is in pain' the statement 'I, P, feel pain.'

The argument that I cannot know that the meanings of the words Guildenstern uses about his experiences correspond with the meanings of those I use about my experiences even though I know that his phonetic acts are of the same type as mine in the given circumstances is not restricted to the issue of the knowledge of other minds. For I cannot know that the meaning of any word one person uses is synonymous with that of any word I use.[2] Here the quest for synonymy and the quest for certainty about the interior of a putative other-person are two sides of the same counterfeit coin. The coin is counterfeit because what is sought is logically impossible, viz. either a rule by which to derive the intension of an expression from its extension or some way to have another person's experience.

What has been established so far is that it is meaningful for me to speak of a human-like entity other than me as being a person, that it is meaningful for me to speak of that entity's experiences. Although I may never be able to *know* anything about the thoughts, feelings, or sensations of another person, it does not follow that for me to assert that I sometimes am able to make true or warranted statements about the contents of another mind is for me to make a meaningless conjecture.

Now, it sometimes is argued that although by the statement 'Guildenstern is in pain' I do not intend a class of statements about Guildenstern's outward behavior or a class of statements about the pain-circumstances of his utterance that he is in pain, there is no reason to be sceptical about his being in pain. For when I assert that he is in pain, my judgment is a conclusion that follows from premisses according to an accepted mode of

---

[2] See Chapter Two, pp. 77-78.

argument. In short, it is maintained that I inductively infer his thoughts or feelings or sensations from his outward behavior and that the inductive method of arguing from the observed to the unobserved is a well-regarded empirical procedure.

I believe that this argument is unsound, for empirical singular statements are in principle candidates for direct and public confirmation. Thus, 'Jones' house is white' is confirmed by seeing a white house that is Jones', and Jones' alone, and the only house owned by Jones. Now, we sometimes assert a statement of this kind without having directly confirmed it, but having directly confirmed other statements. Knowing, for instance, that Jones recently painted his house with the contents of freshly opened paint cans that were labeled 'white', and that such cans almost always contain white paint, and that it is extremely unlikely that he painted his house since that occasion, I may infer and assert that Jones' house is white. The relevant knowledge is inductive support for the statement 'Jones' house is white.' Moreover, I may directly confirm the statement by looking at Jones' house. But is there even in principle a method of directly confirming the statement 'Guildenstern is in pain'? I shall contend that if the paradigm of directly confirming the statement 'Guildenstern is in pain' is Guildenstern's experience of pain together with his recognition of the fact that he is having an experience of pain, then I cannot even in principle directly confirm that he is in pain. For I shall demonstrate that it is logically impossible that anyone other than Guildenstern experience Guildenstern's pain, and consequently that no one but Guildenstern can be in a position directly to confirm any judgment, inductively or otherwise determined, about whether or not he is in pain. And if no one other than Guildenstern can directly confirm the statement that Guildenstern is in pain, then I cannot inductively establish the truth of the assertion that he is in pain, for I cannot be in a position to know independently of his outward behavior and the relevant method of inference whether or not my induction about his feeling or sensation is correct.

But let us consider another argument which sometimes supplements or replaces the inductive argument just stated. It is first asserted that what is to me a statement about another mind, e.g., 'Guildenstern is in pain', is not necessarily a statement about another mind for someone else. It is for Rosencrantz, but not for Guildenstern. It is not legitimate, therefore, to speak about a class of statements that are *only* about other minds. Moreover, Guildenstern can test statements about his experiences which are statements about another mind for the person who makes them; and another person, for instance I, can test statements Guildenstern makes about me, which for him are statements about another mind. It is further alleged by proponents of this doctrine, that Guildenstern can tell me whether or not my statements about his thoughts, feelings, or sensations are true, and that I, conversely, can tell Guildenstern whether or not his statements about my thoughts, feelings, or sensations are true. For instance, when I see Guildenstern's flesh pierced by my foil and hear him cry out and react the way I described, I assert that he is in pain. This assertion is for me about the contents of a putative other-mind, but Guildenstern, about whom it is made, is able to say whether it is true or false, because he can directly inspect his experience and ascertain whether or not a pain-sensation is part of it. He can then say to me, "Yes, I am in pain" or "No, I am not in pain", depending upon which is the case. I no doubt recall occasions on which someone correctly inferred from my behavior that I was in pain. And since the situation in which I now infer that Guildenstern is in pain is analogous to the situations in which someone else inferred that I was in pain, I now conclude that I am correct in believing that Guildenstern is in pain.

But to this argument it sometimes is objected that the assertion that I can test my induction about Guildenstern's alleged state of mind by checking it against his response to my question "Are you in pain?" assumes that my language is the same as his. That is, if I attempt to confirm my inference that Guildenstern is in pain by noting that his response to my question is "Yes, I am in pain", I am assuming that what he means by 'pain' is identical with what I mean by 'pain'. But knowing that Guildenstern's and my use of 'pain' are identical is part of the very problem with which I am confronted. By comparing my language to Guildenstern's, I can discover that we use the same words, i.e., issue the same phonetic acts, in a given situation, even that we use the same words in all situations and that the syntactical structure of our languages is identical, but it does not follow

from this that I can validly infer that our words denote qualitatively identical or even qualitatively similar phenomena. Furthermore, if Guildenstern's words "I am in pain" are taken to be part
of his total response (the way a muscle reaction is part of his
total response), then although I can correctly predict that whenever he is fully conscious and his flesh is pierced he will say "I
am in pain", it does not follow that I am right to conclude that
when he says this he feels what I should denote by the word
'pain'. That our verbal responses coincide or consist of the same
phonetic acts does not entail that our statements have qualitatively identical or even similar referents. Finally, as Wittgenstein
argues,[3] if I know what pain is only from my own experience,
then I know only what *I* call it, not anyone else does.

The belief that I can test my statement that Guildenstern is
in pain by asking him whether he is or is not in pain contributes
a further difficulty to the analysis. My attempt to confirm a
judgment about his pain-sensation by his statement that he is
feeling pain involves the assumption that he is able to hear or to
read my question, to know what kind of feeling or sensation
satisfies the descriptive predicate 'pain-sensation', to recall the
sensation he has had, and to correlate it with words. But how
do I know he can do any of these things? I cannot use the mode
of inference I employ when I infer that Guildenstern is in pain
when he manifests certain outward behavior reactions, because
he does not exhibit any outward signs of pain when he ponders
my question, as he does when he is in pain. And if I have re-
course to a mode of inference different from that which I use to
infer that he is in pain, I should be able to state what it is, how
it may be justified, and why it cannot be used in the first instance
to ascertain whether or not Guildenstern is in pain. But no such
statements are forthcoming, it is alleged.

Let us reflect further on the statement asserted above that
there is no class of statements exclusively about putative other-
minds. According to this assertion, any statement about a putative
person's feelings, thoughts or sensations can be legitimately translated into propositional formulae in accordance with the following method. Given the symbols 'x', 'y', 'z' as name-symbols, and

---

[3] Ludwig Wittgenstein, *Philosophical Investigations*, Sec. 347.

'F' and 'G' as predicate-symbols, and treating predicates as operators that form propositions out of names, we have 'Fx', 'Gx', 'Fy', 'Gy', 'Fz', and 'Gz' as propositional formulae. And given also that 'F' be interpreted as some specific description of a putative person and 'G' as some specific description of a feeling or thought or sensation, we understand the formula 'Fx' & 'Gx', where 'F' is interpreted as 'being some putative person' and 'G' as 'being in pain', as signifying that some putative person is in pain.

Now, the class of possible values for the function 'Fx' is presumed according to the view in question to be equivalent to the class of human beings zoologically determined. If this be so, it follows that the truth of the formula 'Fx & Gx', where 'F' is interpreted as 'being Guildenstern' and 'G' as 'being in pain', is contingent, which is to say that the proposition expressed by the formula and the negation of that proposition are each possible. And it also is contingent, on this view, that someone other than Guildenstern, say Rosencrantz, does not satisfy the function 'Fx'.

Of course, that is not to say that someone other than Guildenstern can satisfy the formula 'Fx & Gx' when it is interpreted as we have interpreted it in the second instance. For 'Fx' was rendered as 'being Guildenstern', and someone can satisfy the formula if and only if he is Guildenstern (and satisfies the remainder of the formula as well). And it is necessarily true that being the person I am, I am not Guildenstern. Assertions like 'If I were you, I should feel your pain' or 'If I were Guildenstern, I should feel his pain' do not, then, refer to a possible situation that as a matter of fact happens not to obtain. Such statements express propositions formed of compound predicators that are logically inconsistent but not meaningless, for instance the predicate 'being Guildenstern and being-not Guildenstern' or the predicate 'being Guildenstern and being myself' (when the predication is made by someone other than Guildenstern). If a compound predicate is well-formed, as these are, it is meaningful even if incapable of empirical exemplification.

May it be said that what is intended by assertions like 'If I were Guildenstern, I should feel his pain' is not that someone should be both himself and someone else, but that if someone other than Guildenstern should satisfy certain descriptions that

Guildenstern in fact satisfies that person would have a sensation of the same sort that Guildenstern is having? Is it not, that is to say, more natural to translate 'If I were Guildenstern, I should feel his pain' into 'If I were in Guildenstern's circumstance, I should be in pain' than into 'If I were identical with Guildenstern, I should feel his pain'?

Now, it may be that when we speak colloquially we mean to say only that if whoever utters the aforementioned hypothetical statement were in Guildenstern's circumstances, he would be in pain, and not that if he were identical with Guildenstern, he would feel his pain. But this is not, I think, what philosophers have intended by the statement 'If I were Guildenstern, I should feel his pain.' Rather, they have intended this by the relevant statement: first, that I should satisfy every description that Guildenstern satisfies at the moment I utter the statement; second, that I should satisfy none of the descriptions that I then satisfy, unless these latter descriptions fortuitously coincide with some that Guildenstern then satisfies; third, that I should satisfy some descriptions; and fourth, that Guildenstern should, when I have satisfied every description that he satisfies at the moment in question, cease to satisfy any description whatever. Their intention, in short, is that I should *be* Guildenstern. And accordingly they assert no more than that Guildenstern feels his own pain and can therefore claim to know that he is in pain. But surely no one questions that Guildenstern can know this. What is questioned is that I can know it. And to identify me with Guildenstern does not solve the problem, but denies that there is a putative other-mind with respect to which there is a problem.

Nor is the colloquial usage of the expression 'If I were Guildenstern, I should feel his pain' any help in deciding the issue. For to interpret the expression as meaning roughly 'If I were in Guildenstern's shoes, I should be in pain' is to rely on inferences made analogically. And the revelant analogy is based on the allegedly question-begging assumption that Guildenstern's and my linguistic usages are identical, or on the failure to recognize that the inferences in question are not ordinary but peculiar in an alleged fatal respect, namely that they cannot be directly confirmed, as other singular empirical statements can.

We have, then, returned to the question 'Can I analogically

infer the contents of a putative other-mind?' But before I analyze
this question directly, I want to consider some relevant sugges-
tions about the general issue whether or not I can have knowledge of the contents of a putative other-mind.

Even if it be granted that my analysis of the general issue is
correct so far as it has gone, can it not be argued that all that
may be meant by the contention that I cannot know that Guildenstern is in pain is that any evidence I adduce to support the
statement that he is in pain is inadequate, where what is meant
by 'inadequate' is that since I cannot experience Guildenstern's
pain, I cannot have evidence of the sort he has for saying he is
in pain? And I cannot have evidence of this sort because, as has
been shown, it is self-contradictory to assert that anyone who
is not Guildenstern can feel Guildenstern's pain. But the self-
contradictoriness refutes the argument itself. For it makes no
sense to speak of my having inadequate evidence for a belief
unless it makes sense to speak of my having adequate evidence
for it. But my having adequate evidence that Guildenstern is in
pain is alleged to be tantamount to my realizing the logically
impossible condition of being both Guildenstern and myself
simultaneously. It follows that in this context it is pointless to
speak either of my having adequate evidence that Guildenstern
is in pain or of my having only inadequate evidence that he is.

Granted then that it is senseless to ask me to have Guildenstern's experience, what are we to make of the statement that his
outward behavior is the best available evidence of his being in
pain? Perhaps what is intended by this statement is that accurate
descriptions of his behavior *constitute* adequate evidence of his
being in pain. Since it has been demonstrated, purely as a matter
of logic, that no one but Guildenstern can feel Guildenstern's
pain, and since logic does not also establish the truth—if it be a
truth—that only Guildenstern can know that he is in pain, it does
seem that his outward behavior is the best available evidence
of his being in pain. Surely this conclusion is credible if one
accepts the proof that it is self-contradictory to demand that I
justify my assertion 'Guildenstern is in pain' by experiencing his
pain.

But clearly, this argument also fails to meet the objection
raised against my inductively inferring what someone's experience

is from my observation of his overt behavior. It does not show how I can tell what Guildenstern's behavior is evidence *for*.

Perhaps, then, although a statement about the experience of a putative other-person is not open to complete or direct testability, it can be unilaterally tested, that is, refuted merely. Consider the following possibility. Suppose Guildenstern gets the sensation I denote by 'pain' whenever he experiences what I denote by 'rapture', and *vice versa*. Since neither of us can have the other's experience and so compare it to his own, how can either of us ever discover the fact we have supposed? Let us be more specific. Suppose I have a severe burning-sensation that I regard as a sufficiently disagreeable pain to want at least to alleviate if not to eliminate entirely. And suppose any feeling of rapture I ever have is something I want to prolong. Accordingly, when I have the severe burning-sensation, my behavior will differ in kind from what it is when I have a feeling of rapture. And if I use 'pain' to denote what Guildenstern uses 'rapture' to denote, and *vice versa,* then he finds it odd that I say I want to alleviate or to eliminate my "rapture", as I find it odd that he says he wants to prolong his disagreeable "pain". If we use 'alleviate', 'eliminate', and 'prolong' identically, what we say points to an inconsistency in our 'pain'-'rapture' usage. The rub is in the 'if'. For the inconsistency may be in our 'alleviate'-'eliminate'-'prolong' usage.

A simpler example is helpful. Consider the similar systematic confusion of 'red' and 'yellow'. If our respective powers to discriminate the experiences denoted by these words from the expereinces denoted by other color words are not impaired, it may seem that we cannot detect the inconsistency in usage. But one of us says that red is darker than yellow, whereas the other says that yellow is darker than red. Hence, our verbal behavior indicates either that we use 'is darker than' differently or that we use 'red' and 'yellow' differently. Which we use differently is ascertained by seeing how we use 'is darker than' in other than 'red'-'yellow' contexts. If we agree, for instance, that blue is darker than pink, that mulberry is darker than lavender, that duck green is darker than baby blue, etc., we likely agree that the difference in question is in our 'red'-'yellow' usage and not in our 'is darker than' usage. Certainly, we should agree that this is so. For if the difference were in our respective usage of 'is

darker than', I should conclude that you experience red and
yellow, but not the other colors, as I do. Hence, I decide that
the inconsistency is in our 'red'-'yellow' usage. Instead of saying
that you experience red and yellow, but not the other colors,
as I do, I say that you experience the others, but not red and
yellow, as I do. Simplicity decides the issue. Quite reasonably,
I make the least necessary adjustment required to achieve consistency.

Do these examples really demonstrate that I can detect an
inconsistency between my usage and a putative other-person's?
The sceptic who denies the possibility of analogical inductive
argument denies that they do, for he points out that by saying
that there is an inconsistency in usages, I assume that the sounds
that issue from the putative other-person are more than mere
noises. I assume that they are issued intentionally; that they are,
and are used as, noises belonging to a certain vocabulary and
conforming to a certain grammar; and that they are used with
a fairly definite sense-and-reference. In short, I assume that the
sounds that issue from the putative other-person are phonetic,
phatic, and rhetic acts; and this entails that the putative other-
person is an agent. For there cannot be an inconsistency here
unless there are two usages; and there cannot be two usages
unless there are two persons, each of whose lingual acts are
phonetically identical but phatically and rhetically different. To
say, then, that there is an inconsistency in usages presupposes
that there are two *persons*.

But what can make the confirmed sceptic believe that a putative other-person is a person? Keep in mind that the confirmed
sceptic rejects any principle of analogical inductive inference as
question-begging. For him the only evidence that a putative
other-person is a person, that is, has experiences, must be something other than the putative other-person's bodily appearance,
for to connect that appearance with an alleged experience of
the body's requires either arguing analogically, or assuming that
the alleged experience is nomologically connected with the
bodily appearance, or linguistically linking the expression that
denotes the alleged experience with the expression that denotes
the bodily appearance. The sceptic maintains that to argue
analogically or to assume that there is a nomological connection

is to beg the question, and that to make the linguistic link is to convert the alleged connection into a logically necessary connection, which *ex hypothesi* it is not. But what evidence does he then demand to justify my contention that a putative other-person has experiences or really is a person? He demands that I have those experiences. For me justifiably to assert that Guildenstern is in pain, the sceptic requires that I have Guildenstern's pain. This, of course, is impossible, so we seem to have reached an impasse. On the one hand, I cannot have a putative other-person's experience; and on the other hand, I seem unable to ascertain what experience his bodily appearance is evidence for, unless I do have that experience.

A fresh start is in order. Notice, to begin with, that it would be improper for me to speak of a putative other-person's *behavior*, for the concept of behavior presupposes interests, desires, intentions, and intelligence, etc.—all of which involve that the putative other-person *is* a person. Hence, we should speak of a putative other-person's *bodily appearance*. And what is at issue is whether or not I can justifiably infer from this appearance, and from changes in it, that the putative other-person undergoes what I call an experience, viz., feels, thinks, or senses something.

Now, 'Guildenstern is in pain' is meaningful in non-philosophical contexts because we ordinarily *assume* that a putative other-person is a person and therefore that he can be in pain. And given this assumption, the question 'How do you know that Guildenstern is in pain?' can be satisfactorily answered by referring to pain-conditions and pain-reactions such as those mentioned in the Guildenstern example. The pain-conditions constitute a context in which the pain-reactions are regarded either as voluntary pain-behavior, e.g. 'I am in pain', or as non-voluntary pain-behavior, e.g. 'Ouch'. The pain-reactions are taken to be either symptoms or a criterion of the putative other-person's being in pain. The difference between a criterion and a symptom is this. Both are phenomena from which we infer that something or other exists or occurs. Thus if we ignore possibly malfunctioning equipment and possible deception, a lighted electric bulb behind the visiting team's hockey goal is the criterion that the home team has just officially scored a goal. But even when a spectator cannot see the bulb, a certain distinctive roar of the crowd may indicate to him that the home team has just officially scored a goal, for he may know that this distinctive roar is correlated with the home team's just having done so. Of course, he can know that this correlation obtains only if he has correlated the roar with the criterion itself. And the difference between the criterion and the symptom is this: If the criterion of something is satisfied, then its being satisfied *logically implies* that the something exists or occurs; but if there is only a symptom of the something, it remains possible that the something does not exist or occur. Thus, in the hockey game example, if the relevant bulb is lighted, a goal officially has been scored by the home team, whereas if the crowd makes its distinctive roar, the goal may not have been scored but they may think it was. The satisfied criterion answers the question 'Has a goal officially been scored?' with certainty. The symptom does not. Without the criterion, the sentence 'The home team just officially scored a goal' would have no use in reporting a hockey game. Given the criterion, the sentence has a use in reporting a hockey game whether or not there is any symptom of the home team's just having officially scored a goal.

Is it justifiable to take a putative other-person's pain-reactions as pain-behavior and to take the pain-behavior as, in certain circumstances, the criterion of his being in pain or a symptom of his being in pain? Surely even the sceptic about knowledge of other minds admits that it makes sense to speak of there being another person, for his denial that I can know that a putative other-person is in pain is a denial that *I* can experience *his* pain, not that the putative other-person can experience pain. The question is then: 'Are the pain-reactions of a putative other-person pain-behavior; and if so, is the pain-behavior, in certain circumstances, the criterion of his being in pain or merely a symptom of his being in pain?' To the first part of this question, the answer is affirmative. The pain-reactions of a putative other-person must be taken as pain-behavior if I am to speak of the possibility of his being in pain. For either I deny the meaningfulness of ascribing pain to a putative other-person or in ascribing it to him, I use 'pain' in connection with the only reactions I have reason to believe are an expression of pain.

What of the contention that if I use 'pain' in connection with

my own pain-experience, then I know only what *I* call an experience of that sort, not what anyone else calls it? This contention puzzles me. A pain is not like a tree, for a pain is not
something I can see, whether it is mine or someone else's. I cannot experience someone else's pain, so the only way I know he
experiences pain is by observing his pain-behavior. Consider this
contention of Strawson's:[4]

> In order for there to be such a concept as that of X's depression, the
> depression which X has, the concept must cover both what is felt,
> but not observed, by X, and what may be observed, but not felt, by
> others than X (for all values of X). But it is perhaps better to say: X's
> depression *is* something, one and the same thing, which is felt, but
> not observed, by X, and observed, but not felt, by others than X. (108-
> 109)

Now, Strawson misses the mark when he writes that a person's
depression can be observed, for surely what can be observed is
not his depression but *that* he is depressed. But given this modification in Strawson's contention, what he writes is instructive: X's
depression *is* something, one and the same thing, that he feels and
I cannot feel, but that I know he feels. What is puzzling about
the contention that my using 'pain' in connection with my own
pain-experience permits me to know only what *I* call an experience of that sort, not what anyone else calls it, is this. I
learn to use the word 'pain' when pain is *ascribed* to me in certain
circumstances. The circumstances are like those described in the
Guildenstern example in that there are noxious stimulation, certain glandular and respiratory reactions, and certain verbal reactions. Notice that some of the circumstances are pain-reactions.
These pain-reactions mediate, so to speak, my putative experience
and the ascriber's ostensive teaching me the use of 'pain'. Nat-
urally, the experience is to me not merely putative. And of course,
what holds my attention is the experience rather than the pain-
reaction or the other circumstances, but sooner or later I notice
these too. And when I do, I too can ascribe pain to a putative
other-person. Ascribing pain to a putative other-person is a way
to explain his pain-reactions and their predictable successors. The
contention that puzzles me misconceives the conceptual grammar

---

[4] P. F. Strawson, *Individuals*, 1959.

of 'pain'. It regards 'pain' as a *straightforward* substantive noun and therefore takes 'Guildenstern is in pain' to be an *ordinary* empirical singular statement. But whereas a straightforward substantive noun, such as 'tree', denotes publicly observable things, 'pain' does not denote anything publicly observable. And similarly, whereas an ordinary empirical singular statement, such as 'There is an oak tree on Guildenstern's front lawn', is directly confirmable by Guildenstern and me, only Guildenstern can even in principle directly confirm the empirical singular statement 'Guildenstern is in pain'. Hence, the word and the statement differ from what they are respectively taken to be. When the puzzling contention takes a pain to be what it is not, it takes the pain to be something known only by the person who has it and it takes 'pain' to be a substantive noun that denotes pains and has its meaning exhausted by its denotation. Consequently, and similarly, when the contention takes the empirical singular statement to be what it is not, it takes it to be confirmable only by the person who has the pain. The puzzle is generated by an ambiguity in the 'known' of the crucial assertion. To say that a pain is something *known* only by the person who has it is tautological insofar as the 'known' is that of experient knowing. But insofar as it is that of scient knowing, not only is the assertion not tautological, it is not even true.

How should a statement ascribing pain to a putative other-person be understood? There are two adequate replies to this question. One account of the ascription is non-criteriological and the other is criteriological. Below, I shall accept the criteriological account because it is better suited to the materialistic conception of mind I defended in the previous chapter but set aside earlier in this chapter for argument's sake.

To understand the noncriteriological account of the ascription, consider the theoretic term 'alpha particle' of physics. An alpha particle is identical with the nucleus of the helium atom and is emitted by a decaying heavy nucleus, such as that of the uranium atom. But an alpha particle is not directly observable. Consequently, it is pointless to attempt a criteriological analysis of it, for instance to say that if something is observed to comprise exactly two protons and two neutrons it is an alpha particle. But it is possible to ascertain the total number of alpha particles emitted in a given time by a radioactive substance, for someone can count the rate at which these particles strike a fluorescent screen that subtends a known angle to the radioactive substance. Then, by permitting all the emitted particles to strike a conductor connected to an electroscope, he can ascertain the charge carried by a known number of particles. This method shows that each alpha particle has a positive charge equal to two electrons. Moreover, streams of these particles can be bent by a strong electric or magnetic field. The ratio of the charge to the mass can be derived from the observed deflection in known fields. And knowing both the charge and its ratio to the mass, the mass of an alpha particle can be derived. This mass is identical with that of the helium atom's.[5]

Notice that the theoretical term 'alpha particle' not only does not denote something observable but is not introduced into the discourse by means of reduction sentences describing experimental conditions whose fulfillment determines its meaning. Rather, it is introduced as part of a theoretical vocabulary used to formulate a theoretical structure and to provide an experimental interpretation of the structure, which interpretation confers empirical meaning on the introduced term.

To clarify this point, consider a standard device for detecting alpha particles, the Wilson cloud chamber. This is a gas-tight chamber (typically a cylinder fitted with a piston at one end and a viewing window at the other), which contains a mixture of gas saturated with the vapor of a liquid, for instance air saturated with alcohol vapor. The piston is withdrawn suddenly, causing the moisture to expand rapidly without time for much heat to flow in. Accordingly, the temperature of the air falls and the air becomes super-saturated and droplets form. This condensation proceeds rapidly only if there are particles in the air to condense onto. These can be dust particles; but if dust particles are not present, condensation will occur on single ions. When an alpha particle passes through the air it ionizes many of the atoms in its path, which form the centers for the condensation of alcohol vapor. Consequently, the ions along the path of the alpha particle

[5] J. D. Stranathan, *The "Particles" of Modern Physics*, 1942, p. 329; F. W. Van Name, Jr., *Modern Physics*, 1952, pp. 256-259; John C. Slater, *Modern Physics*, 1955, pp. 69-72.

become visible as a track of droplets. And a track of a certain
intensity indicates that an alpha particle passed through the air
in the cloud chamber. The intensity of the track of an alpha
particle is greater than that of the track of a beta particle, for
instance.

Now, the presence of a relatively intense track in a Wilson
cloud chamber is not a criterion of the presence of an alpha
particle in the chamber. For the presence of the track does not
logically entail that an alpha particle is present. The presence of
the track is not a necessary and sufficient condition of the presence
of an alpha particle, nor does it specify the meaning of 'alpha
particle'. Rather, the presence of the track merely assigns a partial
empirical content to the term. Moreover, the presence of the
track is not a symptom of the presence of an alpha particle. For
if it were that, then the presence of the track would have to be
correlated with the presence of an alpha particle. But this cannot
be done unless there is some criterion of the presence of the
particle with which the presence of the track can be correlated.
And just as the Wilson cloud chamber cannot provide a criterion,
so neither can a diffusion chamber, nor a scintillation chamber,
nor a spark chamber, etc. We come to understand the meaning
of 'alpha particle' neither by having a *criterion* for its applica-
cation nor by discerning empirical *symptoms* of the appropriate-
ness of its being applied, but by understanding a complex network of lawlike statements in which it appears. This network is
interpretatively connected with observational data, but no reduction sentence or observation sentence can define the theoretical
term.

As 'alpha particle' denotes a theoretical construct that serves,
for instance, to explain scintillations on fluorescent screens and to
predict tracks in a spark chamber, so ' a pain' serves to explain a
pain-reaction and its correlations with other pain-reactions and to
predict other overt reactions, such as the verbal response to the
stimulus-question 'Are you in pain?' The conceptual system of
which 'pain' is part is analogous to the physical theory of which
'alpha particle' is part.[6] 'Pain' is introduced into the discourse as
part of a vocabulary used to formulate a conceptual framework

---

[6] Of course, this is neither to deny that there are also disanalogies nor to
say that 'pain' is *introduced* as an explanatory term.

for, and to provide an experiential interpretation of, the putative personal action described by means of the vocabulary. The vocabulary of which 'pain' is part includes the term 'interest', 'desire', 'motivation', 'intention', and 'satisfaction', etc. Thus, to take a simple example, my concept of *pain* is of something localized at some part of a body, something the putative owner of the body desires to be rid of, something he can rid himself of by making certain intentional movements of his body or by administering drugs to himself or by having certain neural pathways surgically severed, and something whose elimination results in his being satisfied.

Given this analysis of 'pain', it is clear that the issue of meaning that turns on my learning what pain is "from my own case" need not arise. For it is conceivable that I learn what pain is without experiencing it. I may learn what it is by coming to understand 'pain' as it occurs in the network of lawlike statements and in non-lawlike statements. Of course, *ex hypothesis,* I cannot then know what pain is in the experient sense of 'know'. But there is no reason why my knowing it in the scient sense of 'knowing' should depend on my knowing it in the experient sense of 'knowing'.

The other adequate analysis of a statement ascribing pain to a putative other-person is criteriological. In the presence of certain circumstances, such as there being a noxious stimulation, and in the absence of other circumstances, such as the putative other-person's then playing the role of someone hurt in a drama, there are symptoms that the putative other-person is in pain, viz. certain non-voluntary non-verbal reactions, such as the axon reflex; certain non-voluntary verbal reactions, such as his exclaiming 'Ouch'; and certain voluntary verbal reactions, such as 'I am in pain'. The joint occurrence of these reactions (and perhaps also some others), in appropriate circumstances, constitutes the criterion of the putative other-person's being in pain. Notice that the joint occurrence of the relevant reactions is not in itself the criterion of a putative other-person's being in pain, for it is the criterion only *in appropriate circumstances.* The contention is *not* that if the reactions occur jointly, which is to say during a very brief duration, then the putative other-person must be in pain. Rather, the contention is that if the reactions occur jointly in certain circumstances, then the putative other-person must be in pain.

What are the relevant circumstances? There is no point in trying to list them, for they are too numerous and too varied. But the following example illustrates the relevance of circumstances to the pain-reactions' being the criterion of pain-behavior. Suppose I hear a putative other-person groan, see that his face is contorted, hear him blurt out "Help me, I'm in pain", etc. Is he a person in pain? Perhaps not. Perhaps he only pretends to be in pain. His performance may be a mock-performance:—he may be rehearsing for a play or showing how another putative other-person acted. In principle, there are indefinitely many circumstances, such as his pretending, that countervail against the contention that the pain-reactions are pain-behavior. But notice, for instance, that where mock-performance is concerned, the pretender is said to be pretending to be in *pain*. This is important. He is said to be pretending to be in pain because the groaning, the contorted face, the blurted 'Help me, I'm in pain', etc. *are* the criterion of pain-behavior. It is some additional circumstance, such as the putative other-person's saying "I'm only rehearsing for a play" when I try to help him, that makes me say "Oh, you're only pretending to be in pain." Thus, pain-reactions are the criterion of pain-behavior, but whether or not a certain instance of pain-behavior is genuine or feigned depends on the circumstances in which it occurs.

When certain reactions of a putative other-person are rightly taken to be pain-behavior, it may be that the pain-behavior is feigned pain-behavior. But the assertion that it is feigned, that the putative other-person is only pretending to be in pain, presupposes that he is a person, for pretending is something that only a person can do. Thus, given that pain-reactions occur, then despite the possibility that the putative other-person whose reactions they are is not in pain, the pretense-alternative to his really being in pain equally entails that he is a person.

To be sure, since it is logically possible in every instance that the putative other-person who exhibits pain-behavior is only pretending to be in pain, we cannot ever know certainly that he is in pain. But in the absence of any specific countervailing circumstance, the description of those circumstances that do obtain

plus the description of the pain-behavior entail that he is in pain.
Malcolm denies that this is so. He contends, rather, that since the
list of relevant countervailing circumstances is indefinite, there
cannot be any entailment-conditions, any criterion of pain-behavior.[7] He queries: If it does not *follow* from another person's
behavior and circumstances that he is in pain, then how can it
ever be *certain* that he is in pain? Malcolm denies that the conclusion ought to be merely that I cannot 'completely verify' that
the person is in pain, for it is always possible to doubt that he is
in pain.

> The man who doubts the other's pain may be neurotic, may 'lack
> a sense of reality,' but his reasoning is perfectly sound. *If* his doubts
> are true then the injured man is *not* in pain. His [the doubter's] re-
> action is abnormal but not illogical. The certainty that the injured man
> is in pain (the normal reaction) ignores the endless doubts that *could*
> be proposed and investigated. (116)

But Malcolm's query is misleading. From another person's
behavior and circumstances it *does* follow that he is in pain. The
fact that, in any particular instance, the circumstances may differ
from what the doubter takes them to be and may include a
countervailing circumstance of which he is unaware does not
make it less than certain that the person is in pain, unless
'certain' means 'beyond possible doubt'. And if it means that
then what is being urged is that the doubter does not have
certainty because he is uncertain what the circumstances are. But
this is irrelevant to whether or not there can be a criterion of
another person's being in pain. For the criterion exists just in case
certain behavior in certain circumstances entails that the person
is in pain. Whether or not the doubter can or does doubt
that exactly those circumstances obtain is irrelevant to whether
or not a description of them and of the person's pain-behavior
entails that he is in pain. The certainty relevant to the criterion-
issue is a certainty about the *relationship* between that description and the statement that the person is in pain. The certainty
that Malcolm denies his hypothetical doubter is a certainty about
part of the first term in that relationship, namely the description
of the circumstances. Malcolm contends that the doubter cannot

---

[7] Norman Malcolm, *Knowledge and Certainty*, 1963, p. 114.

be certain that the description is accurate, for possibly he is
ignorant of some countervailing circumstance. I agree with
Malcolm that the doubter cannot be certain that another person
is in pain, no matter what the circumstances are in which he
exhibits pain-behavior to the doubter. But Malcolm erroneously
believes that the doubter cannot be certain because no conjunction of circumstances and behavior entails that the person is in
pain. Rather, it is because in no instance can the doubter be certain that the circumstances are what he takes them to be; and
he cannot be certain of his conclusion if he is not certain of his
premises. Contrary to Malcolm's contention, then, the uncertainty about whether or not a person who exhibits pain-behavior
in appropriate circumstances is in pain derives solely from the lack
of complete verification of the premise that describes these
circumstances.

Moreover, Malcolm's comments about the doubter himself are
instructive. According to Malcolm, the doubter's doubt is ab-
normal or neurotic or lacking in a sense of reality, but nevertheless not "illogical". What is the meaning of the word 'illogical'
as Malcolm uses it? Surely not 'unreasonable', for whatever manifests the doubter's lack of a sense of reality *is* unreasonable. 'Self-
contradictory', then. Consequently, the doubt's not being illogical
is tantamount to its being self-consistent. But then Malcolm's
comments do not establish what he takes them to establish.
Suppose I infer from someone's pain-behavior in certain circumstances that he is in pain and the sceptic doubts that the person
is in pain. If his doubt is based merely on the *logical possibility*
that the circumstances are other than I take them to be, I of
course grant that the person *may* not be in pain, but I do not
grant that he *is* not in pain. For the sceptic to give me reason
to grant the latter, he must establish that the circumstances *are*
other than I take them to be in that some specific countervailing
circumstance obtains. It is not enough for him to state the general
thesis that the conditions *may* be other than they are.

The doubter's request for additional justification of my statement that the person who exhibits pain-behavior in certain
circumstances is in pain is legitimate only if he has grounds to
doubt that the person's pain-behavior in those circumstances
itself justifies my belief that he is in pain. When the doubter

questions my conclusion, it is implicit in his questioning that he
has a reason to doubt my conclusion and that I can in principle
remove his doubt by showing that it is unfounded. If this is not
so, there is no point to his asking for additional justification. Thus,
if he alleges that the pain-behavior is a skillful mock-performance,
because the person is anesthetized at the site of noxious stimulation, then in principle I can establish whether or not this allega-
tion is true. What the doubter cannot properly expect is that I
take him seriously before he gives me the reason why he doubts
my conclusion. His doubt is significant only if he has some reason
to doubt. If he objects to my conclusion, it is proper for me to
ask why he objects to it. And if he replies that he has no specific
objection but doubts the conclusion nevertheless or that no matter
how many specific objections I answer he nevertheless will still
doubt the conclusion because there *may* be another objection,
then he shows lack of awareness of a basic characteristic of
reasonable discourse. Justification is associated with specific
criticism, whether actual or possible. If the doubter cannot raise
a specific objection against my conclusion, or cannot give a
reason why he justifiably believes there is some objection that he
himself cannot state, then he cannot reasonably doubt the soundness of my conclusion.

A brief summary is in order. In certain circumstances, certain
of the ongoings of a putative other-person's body are very like
the overt ongoings of my body when I am in pain. These ongoings are called "pain-reactions" to distinguish them from other
reactions of the putative other-person's body. Once it has been
granted that it makes sense for me to speak of a putative other-
person, it is plausible for me to take the pain-reactions of a
putative other-person's body as the overt pain-behavior of a person. For, in appropriate circumstances, these reactions *are prima
facie* pain-behavior, as for instance reactions like mine when I
enjoy a joke I have just been told are *not prima facie* pain
behavior. Since it is logically impossible for me to have someone
else's pain-experience, I must take a putative other-person's bodily
reactions as the only evidence that he is a person. And if the
reactions are pain-reactions, I take them as *prima facie* evidence
that he is a person in pain. To say that a putative other-person
is in pain may be to explain his reactions by using 'pain' as a

theoretical term. Accordingly, 'pain' is part of a theoretical vocabulary that serves to provide a theoretical framework and an experiential interpretation thereof. Or, to say that a putative other-person is in pain may be to say that certain bodily reactions occur in certain circumstances, their joint occurrence in those circumstances being the criterion that the putative other-person is a person in pain, and the occurrence of fewer than all these reactions in these circumstances being symptomatic that he is a person in pain.

Earlier in this chapter I assumed, for the argument's sake, that I do not accept the materialistic conception of mind advocated in Chapter Four. I now reaffirm that theory and link it to knowledge of other minds. The theory dovetails nicely with the second kind of account of an other-mind ascription, the criteriological account. Another-person's being in pain is strictly identical with his body's being in a certain brain-state or undergoing a certain brain-process. And whether or not his body is in such a brain-state or is undergoing such a brain-process is something I can ascertain by examining his body.

Accordingly, my theory is this. The criterion of another-person's being in pain is his body's being in a certain brain-state or undergoing a certain brain-process. In certain circumstances, the joint occurrence of certain of his overt bodily reactions fully justifies my ascribing pain to him; and in these circumstances, the occurrence of fewer than all these bodily reactions is symptomatic of his being in pain but does not fully justify my ascribing pain to him.

Obviously, I can know that someone's being in a certain brain-state or undergoing a certain brain-process is identical with his being in pain only if I can establish a correlation between his pain-reports and the relevant conditions of this body. Since, in fact, too little is known about which brain-states or brain-processes are associated with pain-reports, much less about which specific brain-state or brain-process is associated with which specific pain-report, my theory is advanced as a hypothetical account of mind. And to establish the hypothesis, to learn which brain-states and which brain-processes are associated with which pain-reports, I shall have to take testimony in pain-circumstances. When I see someone in pain-circumstances, I shall have to ask him "Are you in pain", and an affirmative reply will be correlated with his being in a certain brain-state or undergoing a certain brain-process just prior to my asking. Thus, my materialistic theory will be built on such testimony.

To this it may be objected that I then take pain-reports in certain circumstances as my criterion of someone's being in pain, whereas I said that someone's pain-report is only a symptom of his being in pain and that his being in a certain brain-state or undergoing a certain brain-process is the criterion of his being in pain. How do I reconcile the two? As follows. The hypothesis can be established only by regarding testimony, in certain circumstances, as the criterion of the person's being in pain. If extensive and varied experiment establishes the hypothesis, the criterion of someone's being in pain becomes his being in a certain brain-state or undergoing a certain brain-process, and his pain-report becomes only a symptom of his being in pain.

This may seem odd, owing to the fact that a given person's being in pain is something about which he feels he cannot be mistaken in even the smallest detail. Apart from the purely philosophical considerations that show that he can be mistaken,[8] the following empirical examples are useful here. Suppose that someone on whom I have already experimented and about whom I have extensive pain-information reports, at a given moment, that he is then experiencing an *extremely intense,* dull ache in his right forearm. 'Dull' means that the pain's extension is a volume extension rather than an area, linear, or regional extension. 'Extremely intense' means that the pain closely approximates the person's ceiling pain. Now suppose that my previous experimentation has established that, for this person, the pain caused by a stimulus intensity of 248 mc./sec./cm.^{2} has an intensity of two dols. And finally, suppose that his right forearm is being stimulated with a stimulus of that intensity just prior to his reporting, and while he is reporting, that he is experiencing an extremely intense ache in his right forearm. Since 2 dols is far below the intensity of his ceiling pain, which is 10½ dols, I rightly conclude that his ache is not intense but mild. He is mistaken about the intensity of his pain. Moreover, his being in a certain brain-state

---

[8] See Chapter Two, pp. 58-61.

of undergoing a certain brain-process is strictly identical with his feeling a mild ache in his right forearm, his feeling it being correlated with stimuli of 248 mc./sec./cm.^{2} to his right forearm. I thereby correlate his being in that brain-state or undergoing that brain-process with stimuli of 248 mc./sec./cm.^{2} to his right forearm. Gradually I come to use the physiological phenomenon as the criterion of his being in pain and of the pain's having a certain intensity. If he is in the relevant brain-state or is undergoing the relevant brain-process, then he is experiencing a mild ache, not an intense ache, in his right forearm. And accordingly, I discount his report that he is experiencing an extremely intense ache there. Of course, numerous incompatibilities between his pain-reports and the established correlation between intensity of stimuli and his being in certain brain-states or undergoing certain brain-processes lead me to a revised correlation, but that correlation is then the basis for my physiological criterion. If, however, there are but few incompatibilities, then on the occasion of each I hypothesize, for instance, that he is extremely anxious when he estimates the intensity of his ache and therefore overreacts to the ache.

Someone may object that this example shows that the person is mistaken about the intensity of his ache, not about his being in pain. Hence, a second example is in order. Given that I have correlated a person's being in a certain brain-state or undergoing a certain brain-process with his reports of being afraid, then under certain circumstances I justifiably discount his report that he is in pain and point out that his being in the brain-state he is in or his undergoing the brain-process he is undergoing establishes rather that he is afraid.

To conclude then, the issue of whether or not I can have knowledge of another-mind and, if so, of what sort of contents is not to be resolved by proving the principle of analogical inference, but by stating what conditions are appropriate to my accepting such an inference about a putative other-person. It is to be resolved by showing that the sceptic's doubt about the possibility of such knowledge is pseudo-doubt that requires for its expression the possibility of a logically impossible condition, specifically that I be and not be myself. For the sceptic contends that unless I experience a putative person's experience I cannot know that he has any experience and so cannot know that he is a person. Once this contention is seen for what it is, there remains only the task of stating what conditions are taken to be appropriate to my accepting a putative other-person's overt bodily reactions as behavior or action. This task, however, is formidable; and what conditions are appropriate varies with the state of brain physiology.

CHAPTER VI

Knowing and Being Sure

"Pray let us take the air!"
Said the Table to the Chair.

Said the Chair unto the Table,
"Now you *know* we are not able!
"How foolishly you talk,
"When you know we *cannot* walk!"
Said the Table, with a sigh,
"It can do no harm to try . . ."
—EDWARD LEAR, *The Table and the Chair*

Doubt everything at least once . . .
—GEORGE CHRISTOPH LICHTENBERG, *Aphorisms*

The knowledge I shall discuss in this chapter is knowledge of matters of fact or propositional knowledge. Examples of this sort of knowledge are knowledge that there is a red substance on my plate, that there are two meatballs on my plate, that the Empire State Building is taller than the Chrysler Building, that Yosemite National Park is in California, that there are ten letter-tokens in the word 'California', that a 4:30 P.M. eastbound holiday train leaves Pennsylvania Station for Jamaica, New York, that reptiles antedate mammals on the earth, and that the track of an alpha particle is more intense than that of a beta particle. Throughout my discussion I shall use 'p' not as a variable but as an abbreviation for a specific proposition.

Belief is a kind of assurance, the object of which is a proposi-

146

tion. If the negation of a proposition is believed, then the original proposition is disbelieved. A person is more or less strongly inclined to believe a proposition, his inclination to believe it varying from 0% to 100%.[1] When his inclination to believe it is greater than 50% he has a positive inclination to believe it; and when his inclination to believe it is less than 50%, he has a negative inclination to believe it. I shall call a positive inclination simply an inclination, and I shall call a negative inclination a disinclination. A disinclination to believe a proposition, p, of course is not identical with an inclination to believe not-p, for a person can be without an inclination to believe and without an inclination to disbelieve a given proposition. Suppose, for instance, I am asked whether I believe that the next marble drawn from a certain opaque bag will be green or whether I disbelieve it. If I have not seen the contents of the bag and do not know what has previously been drawn from it or what is the percentage of green marbles in the world, etc., then I do not have any inclination either to believe or to disbelieve that the next marble drawn will be green. Rather, I am disinclined to believe that the next marble drawn from the bag will be green and disinclined to disbelieve it. 'Guildenstern believes p' can be explicated dispositionally as 'Guildenstern is prepared to say "Yes" to the question "p?"' and to act as though p were true'; and 'Guildenstern disbelieves p' can be explicated dispositionally as 'Guildenstern is prepared to say "No" to the question "p?"' and to act as though p were false.' Inclination to believe or to disbelieve and disinclination to believe or to disbelieve are epistemic attitudes;[2] and *a belief* is one of these attitudes taken toward a given proposition, the proposition being the content of the belief.

A person may believe a given proposition without having any evidence for it. Although his believing it ordinarily is based on evidence, whether good or poor, he need not have evidence to

---

[1] Cf. C. J. Ducasse, "Propositions, Opinions, Sentences, and Facts", *The Journal of Philosophy*, XXXVII, 26 (1940), pp. 701-711. Following Ducasse, I use the percentages merely as an expository device, without thereby committing myself to the belief that strength of inclination can be quantified.

[2] For expository purposes, I shall ignore the 50% inclination to believe p and the 50% disinclination to believe p, and the 50% inclination to disbelieve p and the 50% disinclination to disbelieve p.

believe it. People frequently believe that certain events will occur or that certain situations obtain and have no reason to believe what they believe other than their desires that the events occur or the situations obtain. Indeed, what sometimes is meant by 'closed-mindedness' is a person's disposition to believe or to disbelieve, in general or on some particular subject, without regard to evidence for or against the truth of the proposition believed or disbelieved. Inclination or disinclination to believe or to disbelieve a given proposition can be more or less rigid or plastic; and if it is utterly rigid, the person whose inclination or disinclination it is believes or disbelieves the proposition no matter what the evidence and no matter that he has no evidence to support his inclination or disinclination to believe or to disbelieve it.

It sometimes is contended that belief differs from *knowledge* in that belief is less than complete conviction whereas knowledge is complete conviction.[3] This contention should be examined. Any person's conviction that a proposition, p, is true is complete if and only if (1) he believes p, and (2) there is no evidence-statement, e, such that if he believes e, then the strength of his inclination to believe p increases. But there can be, and sometimes actually is, a proposition that people do not know to be true but nevertheless have complete conviction about, for instance, among some Christians, the proposition that Jesus of Nazareth was resurrected. These Christians accept that proposition wholly independently of evidential considerations and for them, conseqently, there is no evidence-statement belief of which increases the strength of their respective inclinations to believe the proposition. And although they may say they *know* that he was resurrected, in so saying they use 'know' differently from the way they use it in non-religious contexts, for instance, in the sentences 'I know that there are two meatballs on my plate' and 'I know that the Empire State Building is taller than the Chrysler Building', etc. For these people admit that empirical evidence can in principle be adduced against these latter propositions or their formal contradictories but deny that it can in principle be adduced against the former proposition or its

[3] See, for instance, J. S. Mill, *An Examination of Sir William Hamilton's Philosophy*, 1885, p. 60.

formal contradictory. This difference in usage is crucial and warrants rejecting the contention that knowledge is complete conviction.

It is important to distinguish the possibility of a person's getting additional evidence that a proposition is true from his lack of complete conviction that it is true. For it is self-consistent for a person to admit that additional evidence for the truth of a proposition can be given him and yet to deny that he can be more completely convinced of its truth. Thus, the proposition that I have a tongue can be confirmed by my touching my tongue with one of my fingers and the proposition that I have a head can be confirmed by my looking into a mirror. The consequent tactual and visual sensations would be recorded in sensation-statements that would be genuine evidence statements that I should believe to be true and therefore to support the aforementioned propositions. Yet my conviction that I have a head and that I have a tongue in it would not be more complete than it is now if I were to have the relevant perceptual experiences and were therefore to believe the sensation-statements recording them.

In rejecting the contention that knowledge is identical with complete conviction, I suggested that someone knows that a proposition is true only if he has evidence that it is true. I now want to consider a definition of 'knowledge' that requires that the knower have evidence of the truth of what he knows. Consider the contention that for a person, S, to know a proposition, p, the following conditions must be satisfied: (1) S believes p, (2) S has adequate evidence for p, and (3) p is true. Condition (2) is an abbreviation of three conditions: (2a) S has evidence for p, (2b) S is right about the evidence, and (2c) S is right about the relation of the evidence to p.[4]

The proposed definition is unenlightening because circular. 'Adequate evidence' in (2) means 'propositions known to be true', as is shown by (2b). These propositions, moreover, must be known to stand in a certain logical relationship to p, as is shown by (2c). In short, for S to know p he must have adequate evidence for p, and to have adequate evidence for p, he must

---

4 For such definitions, see for instance Bertrand Russell, *Human Knowledge*, 1948, pp. 154f.; A. D. Woozley, *Theory of Knowledge*, 1949, p. 191; and Roderick Chisholm, *Perceiving*, 1957, p. 16.

know something about a certain set of propositions, e. To understand the meaning of 'S knows p', then, I must already understand the meaning of 'S knows e'; and since knowing p and
knowing e are both instances of propositional knowledge, the
proposed definition is circular.

An alternative definition of 'knowledge' does not require the
knower to have evidence of the truth of what he knows. According to this definition, knowledge is simply correct belief. 'S knows
p if, and only if, (1) S believes p and (2) p is true.' But consider
the following situation. A man who wins a lottery by choosing the
winning number contends he knew what the winning number
would be when he opened his family album and saw both his
father's and his mother's photographs on page seven. He reasoned
that the winning number would be seven times seven, which he
believes to be forty-two. Did he *know* what the winning number
was to be? Or did he only guess what it was to be? Similarly, suppose that a man ascertains the time of day by looking at the face
of a clock that, unknown to him, is not working. And suppose that
when he looks at it, its hands just so happen to give the correct
time. Does the man know the correct time? Or does he coinciden-
tally believe that the time is what it actually is? In asking these
questions, I am distinguishing on the one hand between knowledge and a correct guess, and on the other hand between knowledge and a correct belief. I think there can be no doubt that the
conventions of our actual language include these distinctions, in
short that these conventions do not take correct belief to be
identical with knowledge. Moreover I believe that these distinctions turn on whether or not the believer has good reason to
believe what he believes. Thus, in the first example, someone
may object that the winner only guessed what the winning number was to be, for not only is there no established relationship between photographs in a family album and winning lottery
numbers, but seven times seven is not forty-two. And in the
second example, someone may object that since the clock was not
working, the man could not know what the time was by reading it
off the clock, for a non-working clock does not keep time at all and
hence cannot give the time correctly or even incorrectly. Since
these conventional distinctions are extremely valuable, I want to

reconsider in detail the definition of 'knowledge' I rejected because it is circular.

The definition is this: 'S knows p if, and only if, (1) S believes p, (2) S has adequate evidence for p, and (3) P is true.' The circularity arises if condition (2) is interpreted, as it usually is to require S to know that the evidence-statements are true and that they stand in certain relationship to p. The trouble is caused by the word 'adequate' in (2), for if (2) were (2d) 'S has evidence for p', there would be no circularity, since 'evidence' can be construed as 'statements that S believes to be true and to stand in a certain relationship to p'. But (2d) evidently will not do, for in both the lottery-ticket example and the clock example the subjects believe their respective evidence-statements to be true and to stand in a certain relationship to their respective conclusions. The man who holds the winning lottery-ticket believes that the photographs in his family album are relevant to the winning number and that seven times seven equals forty-two; and the man who looks at the clock believes that it is working properly. Thus, if (2d) were to replace (2) in the definition, I should have to say that each man knows his conclusion, which statement I already had reason to deny. Hence, I reject the proposed substitution.

Merely believing certain evidence-statements, e, to be true is not enough to warrant saying that some proposition, p, is true. In some sense of the word 'adequate', the evidence-statements must constitute adequate evidence for the truth of p. But as I have already pointed out, adequacy of evidence cannot be understood in terms of either knowledge that the evidence-statements are true or knowledge that they stand in a certain relationship to p, for so to understand it is to be guilty of vicious circularity in one's definition.

Perhaps we should understand adequacy as follows. The evidence-statements, e, are adequate evidence for p provided that they do not include any statement, h, that S cannot defend against specific criticism. Accordingly, I replace (2) by (2e), 'S has the right to be sure about p'. Suppose that S asserts the proposition, p, 'The Empire State Building is taller than the Chrysler Building.' Now, if S is asked how he knows p, he may reply (i) that he saw p stated in the current edition of the World Almanac, in the current edition of the Encyclopedia Britannica, and in a current Guide to New York City, each of which is independent of the others; or (ii) that he heard a passerby say just this and no more, "The Empire State Building is taller than the Chrysler Building." Ground (ii) is an utterly unsatisfactory ground for S's saying that he knows p, whereas ground (i) is a satisfactory ground for his saying that he knows p. Ground (ii) can be criticized unanswerably. I can point out to S that he does not have any reason to believe that the passer-by was asserting p, in contradistinction to mentioning it or supposing it, and that even if the passer-by was asserting p, S does not have any reason to believe that the passer-by was correctly informed, as is evident from S's having been misinformed by passers-by about buildings in the city. On the other hand, ground (i) cannot be thus criticized. Of course if I have reason to believe that the three written sources of information contain misprints or that some other reputable sources contain information that contradicts p, then I can properly question the sufficiency of ground (i). An unanswerable objection is one that the person making the knowledge-claim cannot successfully reply to, given the information and techniques he commands. An answerable objection is one that he can successfully reply to, given that information and those techniques.

Not every objection is significant. For an objection to be significant, it must embody a specific doubt that the person making the knowledge-claim can in principle remove by showing it to be unfounded. The critic must state his objection and the specific putative fact(s) on which he bases it. His objection is not significant if his doubt is the general doubt that is expressed in the statement that future evidence may show that any empirical proposition or its formal contradictory is false, although present available evidence indicates that the specific proposition is true and no matter how strongly its truth is now indicated. The reason why an objection of this sort is not significant is that it says nothing about the content of the allegedly known proposition, for it is the nature of any empirical proposition or its formal contradictory to be falsifiable by future experience. Accordingly, the doubt raised by such an objection to an empirical proposition, p, does not differ from the doubt implicit in the affirmation of an *unobjec-*

tionable empirical proposition, q. For in affirming any empirical proposition, a person implies that it may be falsified by future evidence; and so his general objection to p does not differ conceptually from his affirmation of q.

But this concept of adequacy evidently does not suffice. For the mere fact that a person's evidence-statements, e, are defensible against the specific objections raised against them does not guarantee that he has the right to be sure of p. In the lottery-ticket example, for instance, suppose that the only criticism raised against the person's statement that he knew what the winning number was to be is that neither his father's nor his mother's photograph was on page seven of his family album. Suppose further that he shows the critic other photographs that the critic admits to be of the person's father and mother and that he thereby gets the critic to withdraw his objection as mistaken. In the situation described, the claimant to knowledge does reply successfully to the only objection raised against his claim that he knew that the winning number was to be forty-two. Yet it is clear that he did *not* have the right to be sure that the winning number was to be forty-two, that he did *not* know what the winning number was to be. And it is clear just because his evidence-statements, e, were not relevant to the statement, p, that he allegedly derived from them. And they were not relevant whether or not the objection of irrelevance is raised against them. Whether or not someone knows a proposition does not depend on the relative ignorance of critics, so that if their criticism is slight and therefore easily answered by the claimant to knowledge, he is credited with knowing what he claims to know.

Perhaps, then, we should stipulate that the objections against which the claimant be required to defend his claim to know p be such as would be raised by someone sufficiently well-informed to hold all relevant beliefs. A belief, q, is relevant to knowledge that p if S's knowing p either presupposes or entails q. Thus, in the lottery-ticket example, the proposition, q, that seven times seven equals forty-two is presupposed by S's (allegedly) knowing p; and since q is false, it follows that S does not know p. The rub, of course, is in the word 'all'. For when are we entitled to say that the objections are such as would be raised by someone sufficiently well-informed to hold *all* relevant beliefs? Clearly 'all

relevant beliefs' does not mean 'all logically possible beliefs
having some bearing on S's knowing p', for at no time can anyone
justifiably exclude the possibility that future experience will lead
someone to a belief no one now holds that bears on S's knowing
p. Rather, it means 'the sum total of relevant beliefs held at the
time S claims to know p'. But then, can we ascertain that the
objections against which S successfully defends his claim to know
p are such as would be raised by someone sufficiently well-
informed to hold the sum total of relevant beliefs held by any
and all persons living when S claims to know p? Or is this condition one that we cannot ascertain to be satisfied but must
regard as asymptotically approached?

To begin with, however, notice that whichever is the case,
'adequate' has been defined and consequently so has 'S knows p'.
The latter is true if, and only if, (1) S believes p, (2) when he
claims to know p, S can defend his claim that p is true by pre-
senting evidence for p and by defending his claim that p is true
against any objection that would then be raised by someone
sufficiently well-informed to hold all beliefs relevant to p, and
(3) p is true. 'Knowledge' can then be defined as 'any given person's correct belief that a proposition is true (or false) plus his
having adequate evidence that the proposition is what he believes
it to be'.

Now, I think that a person(s) can ascertain that the objections
against which a given person, S, successfully defends his claim
to know a proposition, p, are such as would be raised by someone
sufficiently well-informed to hold the sum total of relevant beliefs
held by any and all persons living when S claims to know p.
Consider a simple model of the knowledge-situation. Suppose S
claims to know that a certain book has fewer than three hundred
pages and that he claims to know this because he read the book
and recognized that everything its preface states it will cover is
covered by the end of its last page, which is two hundred and
ninety-eight. Suppose now that someone objects that S does not
know p, because two or more pages may have been torn from
the book, which pages summarize what has been stated on the
first two hundred and ninety-eight pages. Suppose finally that S
and this person examine the book and agree on the basis of their
examination that no page has been torn from the book. If every-

one is made aware of the situation just described and no one
raises any further objection upon being asked to raise whatever
objection he can, then the objections against which S has successfully defended his claim to know p are such as would be
raised by someone sufficiently well-informed to hold the sum
total of relevant beliefs held by any and all persons living when
S claims to know p. The content of this model knowledge-situation is much simpler than that of most knowledge-situations and
its claim to knowledge is easier to defend successfully and to
ascertain to be successfully defended than are those of most
knowledge-situations. But the logical structure of the complex
knowledge-situations is identical with that of the simple knowledge-situation.

Now there is a familiar objection to this account of knowledge,
namely that it seems to require the claimant to defend his claim
to know a proposition, p, by adducing as evidence for p some
further proposition(s), e, that he knows. And if the account does
require this, then it does not eliminate the circularity that was to
be eliminated by substituting (2e) for (2) and interpreting it as
I interpreted it. Rather, the account then commits its advocate to
a vicious infinite regress.

I believe that this objection is mistaken, not because it is
argued invalidly but because its major premise is false. The account does *not* require the claimant to defend his claim to know
a proposition, p, by adducing as evidence for p some further
proposition(s), e, that he knows. What entitles S to be sure about
p is not his being able to state e, or his being able to state e and
that e warrants p, but his having had certain experiences. As
Peirce[5] writes:

> . . . in every state of intellectual development and of information, there
> are things that seem to us sure, because no little ingenuity and reflec-
> tion is needed to see how anything can be false which all our previous
> experience seems to support; so that even though we tell ourselves
> we are *not* sure, we cannot clearly see *how* we fail of being so. (4.64)

If, for instance, S sees a book on his desk and the book looks
familiar to him, then provided I am not in a position to see for

---

[5] Charles Sanders Peirce, *Collected Papers*, Edited by Charles Hartshorne
and Paul Weiss, 1933.

myself, he may give evidence to me that there is a book on his
desk by asserting the proposition, p, 'There is a book on my desk.'
But he does not thereby give evidence to himself that the book is
there. Nor need he, for he actually sees it there. In a preceptual
situation such as that in which he finds himself, there can be no
meaningful question of his giving evidence or having evidence
that p, unless there is some reason to doubt that he sees a book
on the desk. That he may be wrong about there being a book on
his desk is not the point. Any claim to empirical knowledge may
be mistaken. And if S is wrong about there being a book on his
desk, his claim is voided. For one condition of anyone's knowing
p is that p is true. But despite p's being false, S may have the
right to be sure of p. At any event, there are no ultimate or
absolutely indubitable propositions on which a knowledge-claim
necessarily rests, neither metaphysical propositions nor empirical
propositions. A knowledge-claim has only to start with propositions free from actual doubt.[6] And *genuine* doubt, it should be
remembered,

> cannot be created by a mere effort of will, but must be compassed
> through experience; . . . [and] in so far as we do not doubt a prop-
> osition we cannot but regard it as perfectly true and perfectly
> certain. . . .[7]

As Peirce remarks,

> genuine doubt always has an external origin, usually from surprise
> (5.443). A true doubt is accordingly a doubt which really interferes
> with the smooth working of the [relevant] belief-habit, . . . [which
> interferes with the doubter's] natural mode of acting (5.510).

Giving evidence, then, is an effortful reaction to the resistance of
genuine doubt; and when there is no genuine doubt about the
truth of a given proposition, p, there is no point in giving evidence for p.

The account of knowledge, then, is this. A person, S knows a
proposition, p, if and only if (1) S believes p, (2) S has the right
to be sure that p, and (3) p is true.

---

[6] See Chapter Two, pp. 58-61. Cf. Charles Sanders Peirce, *Collected Papers,*
Edited by Charles Hartshorne and Paul Weiss, 1934, 5.376; and J. L. Austin,
Sense and Sensibilia, 1962, Lecture X.

[7] Charles Sanders Peirce, *op. cit.,* 5.498.

There is, however, yet another objection that someone may raise against this account of knowledge. I explicated the right to be sure of a given proposition, p, in terms of successfully defending a knowledge-claim against actual objections. And the success is determined according to a standard of evidence that the claimant and the critic share. But suppose that a critic, C, objects to the standard of evidence according to which a person, S, claims to know a proposition, p. C contends that S does not know p, but contends this neither because S allegedly does not believe p nor because p allegedly is false, but because S's evidence-statements fail to meet C's more stringent standard of evidence. Thus, a natural scientist, for instance, may refuse to accept any historical causal proposition as known, because unlike scientific causal propositions, historical causal propositions are not derived from investigation of repeatable situations but of unique situations. Natural sciences are concerned with types of occurrences, numerous instances of which can be investigated, whereas history is concerned with particular occurrences, each of which is unique. C alleges that repeatability is necessary if a situation is to be causally explained; and so historical causal propositions, which do not concern repeatable situations, are unknowable in principle. In short, he contends that the concept *knowledge of an historical causal proposition* is self-contradictory or senseless. What he thereby attempts to exclude from the category of even possible knowledge are statements such as the following. (A) Towards the end of the eleventh century, four factors combined to produce the movement known as the crusade: (1) a growing feudal aristocracy in France that tended to swarm into surrounding regions, (2) a reformed papacy that ardently laid claim to the moral leadership of Europe, (3) a great commercial revival that brought to old cities a new population eager for mercantile expansion, and (4) the rise of a Turkish power that overran the Byzantine Empire. (B) Had it not been for the appeal of Pope Urban II, there would not have been a crusade.[8] What are we to make of a dispute about the standard of evidence itself?

We cannot merely point out that one standard of evidence more closely approximates common usages than does the other, for

---

[8] Carl Stephenson, *Mediaeval History*, 3rd edit., 1951, pp. 227-230.

what is in dispute is the standards themselves, not whether or not they accord with common usage. The decision to accept one of exclusive alternative standards of evidence is arbitrary in that no statement can justify the decision either deductively or inductively. But the decision is also non-arbitrary in that it has an experiential underpinning in each disputant's unique body of experiences. Given that the aforementioned critic affirms a certain standard of evidence incompatible with ours, we may urge that his statement requires him to reject particular statements as non-knowledge, which statements he in fact regards as knowledge, and that he therefore is guilty of an inconsistency. If we do this, it is then up to him to decide whether to renounce his standard or to reject the statements. And if he rejects the statements, thereby making his "knowledge" consistent with his standard, it remains for us only to accept or to reject his standard. The issue now is purely terminological. The critic's standard may be an acceptable (or a non-acceptable) verbal innovation, but whether it is acceptable or not is a matter of personal preference.

Epilogue

"Are we nearly there?" Alice managed to pant out at last.

"Nearly there!" the Queen repeated. "Why, we passed it ten minutes ago!"
—Lewis Carroll, *Through the Looking-Glass*

Philosophy is a peculiar mixture of describing, evaluating, and prescribing. The philosopher works within a tradition about which he reflects critically and from which he diverges when the cogency of argument compels him to disagree. He is usually merely "an under-laborer . . . clearing the ground a little, and removing some of the rubbish that lies in the way of knowledge . . ."[1] Each time he recognizes and removes a piece of rubbish, the path to knowledge becomes easier to walk.

I have been discussing a cluster of intimately connected epistemological problems. In proposing solutions to these problems, I have not only recognized and removed some rubbish, but have illuminated epistemological discourse itself.

---

[1] John Locke, *An Essay Concerning Human Understanding*, 1690, "Epistle to the Reader."

Bibliography*

Anscombe, G. E. M., *An Introduction to Wittgenstein's Tractatus*, Hutchinson University Library, 1958.

Aristotle, *Topics*.

Armstrong, D. M., "Is Introspective Knowledge Incorrigible?", *The Philosophical Review*, 1963, pp. 417-432.

Austin, J. L., *How To Do Things With Words*, Oxford University Press, 1962.

Austin, J. L., *Sense and Sensibilia*, Oxford University Press, 1962.

Ayer, A. J., "Can There Be A Private Language?", in *Aristotelian Society Supplementary Volume XXVIII*, Harrison & Sons, Ltd., 1954.

Ayer, A. J., *The Concept of A Person*, St. Martin's Press, Inc., 1963.

Ayer, A. J., *The Problem of Knowledge*, Macmillan & Co. Ltd, 1956.

Barnes, Winston H. F., *The Philosophical Predicament*, Adam and Charles Black, 1950.

Black, Max, *Language and Philosophy*, Cornell University Press, 1949.

Blanshard, Brand, *Reason and Analysis*, Open Court Publishing Company, 1962.

Boas, George, *The Inquiring Mind*, Open Court Publishing Company, 1959.

Bradley, R. D., "Avowals of Immediate Experience", *Mind*, 1964, pp. 186-203.

Braithwaite, Richard Bevan, *Scientific Explanation*, Cambridge University Press, 1953.

Britton, Karl, *Communication*, Harcourt, Brace and Company, 1939.

Broad, C. D., *Lectures on Psychical Research*, The Humanities Press, 1962.

Carnap, Rudolph, *The Logical Syntax of Language*, Routledge & Kegan Paul Ltd., 1937.

Carney, James D., "Private Language: The Logic of Wittgenstein's Argument", *Mind*, 1960, pp. 560-565.

Castaneda, Hector-Neri, "Criteria, Analogy, and Knowledge of Other Minds", *The Journal of Philosophy*, 1962, pp. 533-546.

Cherniss, Harold, "The Philosophical Economy of the Theory of Ideas", *American Journal of Philology*, 1936.

160

Chisholm, Roderick, *Perceiving*, Cornell University Press, 1957.

Cornman, James W., "The Identity of Mind and Body", *The Journal of Philosophy*, 1962, pp. 486-492.

Ducasse, C. J., *Nature, Mind, and Death*, Open Court Publishing Company, 1951.

Ducasse, C. J., "Propositions, Opinions, Sentences, and Facts", *The Journal of Philosophy*, 1940, pp. 701-711.

Eddington, A. S., *The Nature of the Physical World*, The Macmillan Company, 1929.

Feigl, Herbert, "The 'Mental' and the 'Physical' ", in Herbert Feigl, Michael Scriven and Grover Maxwell, eds., *Minnesota Studies in the Philosophy of Science*, Volume II, University of Minnesota Press, 1958.

Feigl, Herbert, "Other Minds and the Egocentric Predicament", *The Journal of Philosophy*, 1958, pp. 978-987.

Findlay, J. N., *Language, Mind, and Value*, Humanities Press, 1955.

Flew, Antony, "Philosophy and Language", in Antony Flew, ed., *Essays in Conceptual Analysis*, Macmillan & Co. Ltd., 1956.

Fox, Oliver, *Astral Projection*, University Books Inc., 1962.

Geach, Peter, *Mental Acts*, Routledge & Kegan Paul Ltd, 1957.

Hall, Everett W., *Our Knowledge of Fact and Value*, University of North Carolina Press, 1961.

Hall, Everett W., *Philosophical Systems*, University of Chicago Press, 1960.

Hampshire, Stuart, "The Interpretation of Language: Words and Concepts", in C. A. Mace, ed., *British Philosophy in the Mid-Century*, The Macmillan Company, 1957.

Hampshire, Stuart, *Thought and Action*, The Viking Press, 1960.

Hanson, Norwood Russell, *Patterns of Discovery*, Cambridge University Press, 1958.

Hintikka, Jaako, "On Wittgenstein's 'Solipsism' ", *Mind*, 1958.

Hoffman, Robert, "Conjectures and Refutations on the Ontological Status of the Work of Art", *Mind*, 1962, pp. 512-520.

Hook, Sidney, ed., *Dimensions of Mind*, New York University Press, 1960.

Hume, David, *An Enquiry concerning Human Understanding* (Posthumous Edition of 1777), ed. by L. A. Selby-Bigge, 2nd edit., Oxford University Press, 1902.

Isaacs, Nathan, "What Do Linguistic Philohsophers Assume?", *Proceedings of the Aristotelian Society*, 1955-1956, Harrison & Sons, Ltd., 1956.

Johnstone, Henry W., Jr., *Philosophy and Argument*, The Pennsylvania State University Press, 1959.

Korner, Stephen, *Conceptual Thinking*, Cambridge University Press, 1955.

Lashley, K. S., "In Search of the Engram", *Symposia of the Society of Experimental Biology*, 1950.

Levinson, A. B., "Waismann on Proof and Philosophical Argument", *Mind*, 1964, pp. 111-116.

Linsky, Leonard, "On Ceasing to Exist", *Mind*, 1960, pp. 249-250.

Locke, John, *An Essay Concerning Human Understanding*, 1690.

Malcolm, Norman, *Knowledge and Certainty*, Prentice-Hall Inc., 1963.

Malcolm, Norman, "Scientific Materialism and the Identity Theory", *Dialogue*, 1964, pp. 115-125.

Melden, A. I., *Free Action*, Routledge & Kegan Paul, 1961.

Mill, J. S., *An Examination of Sir William Hamilton's Philosophy*, Longman, Roberts & Green, 1885.

Moore, George Edward, *Commonplace Book, 1919-1953*, ed. by Casimir Lewy, George Allen & Unwin Ltd, 1962.

Moore, George Edward, *Philosophical Papers*, George Allen & Unwin Ltd, 1959.

Moore, George Edward, *Some Main Problems of Philosophy*, George Allen & Unwin Ltd., 1953.

Nidditch, P. H., *Introductory Formal Logic of Mathematics*, The Free Press, 1957.

Pap, Arthur, *Elements of Analytic Philosophy*, The Macmillian Company, 1949.

Passmore, John, *A Hundred Years of Philosophy*, The Macmillan Company, 1957.

Passmore, John, *Philosophical Reasoning*, Charles Scribner's Sons, 1961.

Pears, D. F., ed., *David Hume*, Macmillan & Co. Ltd, 1963.

Peirce, Charles Sanders, *Collected Papers*, ed. by Charles Hartshorne and Paul Weiss, Harvard University Press, Volumes 4 and 5, 1933 and 1934.

Pitcher, George, *The Philosophy of Wittgenstein*, Prentice-Hall Inc., 1964.

Popper, Karl R., *Conjectures and Refutations*, Basic Books, 1962.

Reichenbach, Hans, *Experience and Prediction*, The University of Chicago Press, 1937.

Rhees, R., "Can There Be A Private Language?", in *Aristotelian Society Supplementary Volume XXVIII*, Harrison & Sons, Ltd., 1954.

Russell, Bertrand, *Human Knowledge: Its Scope and Limits*, Simon and Schuster, 1948.

Russell, Bertrand, "On Scientific Method in Philosophy", in *Mysticism and Logic*, George Allen & Unwin Ltd, 1917.

Russell, Bertrand, *The Principles of Mathematics*, 2nd edit., George Allen & Unwin Ltd, 1937.

Ryle, Gilbert, *The Concept of Mind*, Barnes & Noble, Inc., 1949.

Schlesinger, G., *Method in Physical Science*, The Humanities Press, 1963.

Sellars, Wilfrid, *Science, Perception and Reality*, The Humanities Press, 1963.

Shaffer, Jerome, "Could Mental States Be Brain Processes?", *The Journal of Philosophy*, 1961, pp. 813-822.

Slater, John C., *Modern Physics*, McGraw-Hill Book Company, Inc., 1955.

Smart, J. J. C., "Sensations and Brain Processes", *The Philosophical Review*, 1959, pp. 141-156.

Smart, J. J. C., *Philosophy and Scientific Realism*, Routledge & Kegan Paul, 1963.

Spinoza, Benedictus de, *Ethics*.

Stebbing, L. Susan, *Philosophy and the Physicists* (1937), Dover Publications, Inc., 1958.

Stephenson, Carl, *Mediaeval History*, 3rd edit., Harper & Brothers, 1951.

Stranathan, J. D., *The "Particles" of Modern Physics*, The Blakiston Company, Inc., 1942.

Strawson, P. F., *Individuals*, Methuen & Co Ltd, 1959.

Tanburn, N. P., "Private Languages Again", *Mind*, 1963, pp. 88-102.

Thomson, Judith Jarvis, "Private Languages", *American Philosophical Quarterly*, 1964, pp. 20-31.

Thorpe, W. H., *Learning and Instinct in Animals*, Harvard University Press, 1956.

Todd, William, "Private Languages", *The Philosophical Quarterly*, 1962, pp. 206-217.

Toulmin, Stephen Edelston, *The Uses of Argument*, Cambridge University Press, 1958.

Urmson, J. O., "Recognition", *Proceedings of the Aristotelian Society*, 1955-1956, Harrison & Sons, Ltd., 1956.

Van Name Jr., F. W., *Modern Physics*, Prentice-Hall, Inc., 1952.

Waismann, Friedrich, "How I See Philosophy", in H. D. Lewis, ed., *Contemporary British Philosophy*, George Allen & Unwin Ltd, 1956.

Walsh, W. H., *Metaphysics*, Hutchinson University Library, 1963.

Weisskopf, Victor F., *Knowledge and Wonder*, Doubleday & Company, Inc., 1963.

Wellman, Carl, "Wittgenstein and the Egocentric Predicament", *Mind*, 1959, pp. 223-233.

Wellman, Carl, "Wittgenstein's Conception of a Criterion", *The Philosophical Review*, 1962, pp. 433-447.

White, Morton, *Toward Reunion in Philosophy*, Harvard University Press, 1956.

Whiteley, C. H., *An Introduction to Metaphysics* (1950), reprinted with corrections, Methuen & Co. Ltd., 1955.

Wittgenstein, Ludwig, *Notebooks 1914-1916*, trans. by G. E. M. Anscombe, Harper & Brothers, 1961.

Wittgenstein, Ludwig, *Philosophical Investigations*, 2nd edit., trans. by G. E. M. Anscombe, Basil Blackwell, 1958.

Wittgenstein, Ludwig, *Tractatus Logico-Philosophicus* (1921), trans. by D. F. Pears & B. F. McGuiness, The Humanities Press, 1961.

Woozley, A. D., *Theory of Knowledge*, Hutchinson University Library, 1949.

Zimmer, Ernest, *The Revolution in Physics,* trans. by H. Stafford Hatfield, The Macmillan Company, no date.

* No work published after July 1964 was read before writing this book.

Index

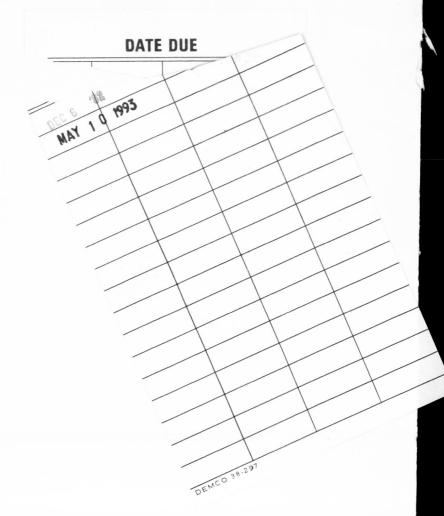